COCONUT OIL

Quarto is the authority on a wide range of topics.

Quarto educates, entertains and enriches the lives of
our readers – enthusiasts and lovers of hands-on living.

www.QuartoKnows.com

First published in the UK in 2017 by

Apple Press

74–77 White Lion Street

London N1 9PF

United Kingdom

Copyright © 2017

Quintet Publishing Limited

Ovest House,

58 West Street,

Brighton

East Sussex

BN1 2RA

QTT.1COC

ISBN: 978-1-84543-679-7

Designers: Lucy Parissi & Bonnie Bryan

Photographers: Lucy Parissi & Emma Gutteridge

Art Director: Michael Charles

Project Editor: Cara Frost-Sharratt

Editorial Director: Emma Bastow

Publisher: Mark Searle

Printed in China

2 4 6 8 10 9 7 5 3 1

COCONUT

OIL

**Over 200 easy recipes and uses
for home, health and beauty**

Laura Agar Wilson

APPLE PRESS

Laura Agar Wilson is a health and lifestyle coach certified with the Institute of Integrative Nutrition and registered with the Federation of Holistic Therapists.

As a blogger, wellness writer, and recipe developer featured in publications such as *Superfood Magazine, Gurgle, Natural Health Magazine,* and *The Telegraph,* Laura is passionate about making healthy living more accessible and achievable.

In 2009 she founded her blog wholeheartedlyhealthy.com to help empower women to live healthier, happier, and more balanced lives.

Laura lives in Durham, UK, with her husband James and son Finley.

Contents

Introduction

In recent years, the western world has experienced a major shift in its approach to health and wellbeing. Where we were once advised to cut down on fat and sold the benefits of refined foods, we are now experiencing a complete turnaround and something of a dietary revolution.

As we move towards a more natural diet, coconut oil has emerged as a hero food and a staple in the diets of health-conscious eaters. Having previously been regarded as an unhealthy ingredient due to its high levels of fat, its many health benefits are now being rediscovered.

The real wonder of coconut oil is its versatility: as well as its known uses in cooking, it has many applications that can support health and natural beauty and it can also be used around the home.

History of coconut oil

The coconut is the fruit of the palm *Cocos nucifera* and it is a remarkable member of the plant kingdom. The compact shell contains food (the flesh) and hydration in the form of coconut water. And, once you've consumed the contents, the shell itself can prove extremely useful: it can be burnt as fuel, turned into charcoal or used as a bowl.

It's no surprise then, that coconuts have played a major role throughout human history – they were first documented in Sanskrit literature in the 4th century BC. They were also transported on the world's first trade ships across the Pacific.

Inhabitants of the Indian Ocean and Pacific Islands were already well aware of the diverse uses of the coconut and, once trading routes were established, it wasn't long before ships were laden down with the exotic fruit.

Later, coconuts were used during World War I, when their shells were charred to create charcoal to be used in gas masks. In World War II coconut water was used in emergency transfusions in the absence of plasma, as coconut water has the same electrolyte balance as human blood.

However, when links were made in the late 1980s between dietary fat – particularly saturated fat – and blood cholesterol, coconut oil 'butters' and 'margarines' were removed from shopping baskets and replaced with products containing fillers and additives that were designed to lower saturated fat content.

Fast-forward a few years and our view of fat has completely changed. It's now recognised that fat in moderation isn't the enemy: in many cases it is actually essential to good health and, when it comes to coconut oil, there are lots of other benefits as well.

As a result of this change in attitude, coconut oil is more popular than ever and is now widely available and sits on the shelves of most supermarkets around the world.

Health benefits

The secret to coconut oil's remarkable health benefits lies in its unique fat profile. Unlike most other saturated fats, which have long-chain fatty acids, coconut oil contains medium-chain fatty acids, which behave differently in the body: they are quickly absorbed and easy to digest, making them an excellent source of energy. Plus, they aren't automatically stored as fat in the same way as other fatty acids. So coconut oil is the ideal way to consume 'good' fats but it has many other reputed health benefits, too.

Increases metabolism

Coconut oil is a thermogenic food, which means it increases the rate that your body burns energy in comparison to other fats.

Decreases appetite to support weight loss

The high fat content can help to decrease appetite and balance blood sugar levels.

Can support heart health

The antioxidant value of coconut oil has also been linked with lowered blood pressure via decreased oxidative stress.

Source of energy

The fatty acids in coconut oil are taken directly to the liver, where they are quickly metabolised into energy and sent to the muscles to be used.

Improves endurance

As coconut oil provides energy in the form of fat that is more slowly digested than carbohydrate sources, it can support endurance.

Antibacterial, antiviral and antifungal

These properties are a result of the lauric acid content. Lauric acid is converted to monolaurin, a substance with antiviral and antibacterial properties.

Anti-inflammatory properties

Coconut oil can have an anti-inflammatory effect within the body, supporting the symptoms of arthritis and other inflammation.

Improves digestion

Coconut oil can improve digestion by supporting gut health through the reduction of bad bacteria – such as candida – that can lead to bloating, inflammation and pain.

Supports the immune system

Due to coconut oil's antibacterial, antifungal and antiviral properties, it reduces the stress on the body's immune system, supporting it to be more effective in fighting diseases.

Antioxidant

Coconut oil contains compounds that act as antioxidants within the body.

Supports vitamin and mineral absorption

Vitamins such as A, D, E and K are fat-soluble, which means that they need to be ingested with a source of fat: coconut oil is an excellent choice.

Helps fight gum disease

The antibacterial benefits of coconut oil can help to remove bacteria from the mouth (which can cause gum disease), as well as support the healing of gums.

Modern production

Not all coconut oil is equal and this largely comes down to how the coconut is grown and how the oil is produced.

Coconuts are in season all year and grow in clusters of 5 to 12. They turn from a new flower to a fully mature nut in around 12 months. When they're ready they naturally drop to the ground and most quality producers will wait to harvest their coconuts as close to full maturity as possible.

Coconut oil itself comes from the white flesh of the coconut and there are two main ways that coconut oil is produced. The first method involves drying the coconut flesh into something known as copra. The second also dries the coconut flesh but the oil is then extracted in a different way to produce virgin or extra virgin coconut oil.

In copra production the flesh is dried in a kiln, on a rack over a fire or under the sun. The copra is then taken to a facility where the oil is extracted. The transportation can damage the copra and it can become rancid and grow mould, so it needs to be refined through procedures such as bleaching and deodorising to make it edible. This results in refined, bleached and deodorised (RBD) oil – a poorer quality oil that has fewer health properties.

The second production method can involve drying the white coconut flesh, or using it raw.

The high fat content in coconut oil can help to decrease appetite and to balance blood sugar levels.

Rather than transporting it to be refined, the coconut oil is produced through one of the following methods:

Centrifuge: The oil is separated from the coconut milk, which is made by soaking grated coconut flesh in hot water. The coconut milk is then passed through a centrifuge.

Fermenting: This method also uses coconut milk, which is heated and left overnight for the coconut milk to separate into different solids and oils. This is the traditional method of production.

Direct micro-expelling: A method designed for small village businesses, it involves the coconut being dried for 30 minutes then being loaded into a manually operated press to extract the oil.

Expeller pressed: This method can be performed either cold or warm and involves the coconut flesh being lightly dried then pressed, to extract the oil.

Some methods use heat to assist the process and extract more oil, whereas other methods cool the equipment with water to ensure a cold-pressed product.

All these methods produce virgin or extra virgin coconut oil. Currently there are no industry standards that dictate what is virgin or extra virgin, so these terms mean the same thing.

As well as refined coconut oil and virgin or extra virgin oil production, some other forms of coconut oil also exist:

Hydrogenated coconut oil: Coconut oil that has been chemically altered from refined coconut oil. Due to this alteration it has become a trans fat and is often used in the production of processed foods.

Fractionated coconut oil: This is coconut oil that has been split into its different types of fat. Unlike other forms of coconut oil, fractionated coconut oil is liquid at room temperature.

Buying guide

Due to the popularity of coconut oil, there are now many different brands and varieties available – with various descriptions and claims – which can make it difficult to choose.

Here's what many of the product descriptions actually mean:

• **Organic:** The coconuts used to produce the oil have not been treated with chemical fertilisers or pesticides. Look for organic certification.

• **Virgin coconut oil:** Coconut oil that has not been refined (this means the same as extra virgin).

• **Extra virgin coconut oil:** Coconut oil that has not been refined (the same as virgin coconut oil).

• **Unrefined coconut oil:** The coconut oil has not been chemically treated, fractionated, bleached or deodorised.

• **Refined coconut oil:** A coconut oil produced using the copra method, which has undergone boiling, chemical bleaching and deodorising.

• **Raw:** The coconut oil has been produced without using temperatures over 45°C (113°F).

• **Cold/wet milled:** The coconut oil has been produced without heat; using cold water for the extraction process.

• **Odourless:** The coconut oil has been steamed or otherwise processed to remove the coconut taste and smell.

• **Fractionated coconut oil:** Coconut oil that has had some of its fatty acids removed; most often the lauric acid. Sometimes labelled MCT oil, depending on which fatty acids remain.

What to look for

Coconut oil should be solid at room temperature with a melting point of 24°C (76°F). A good quality oil should be white when solid and completely clear when liquid: there should be no discolouration. It should smell fresh with a light coconut aroma. When you rub the oil between your fingers it should feel smooth with no grittiness. Coconut oil is best stored in a glass jar, so look for products in glass containers rather than plastic.

Choosing your oil

Different uses do not generally require a different type of oil. For most of the recipes and preparations in this book I recommend purchasing unrefined virgin or extra virgin coconut oil – choose organic, where possible. It's not essential to choose a raw, cold/wet milled coconut oil but these oils are the best possible quality and will therefore offer the greatest benefits.

I only recommend refined coconut oil for certain applications, such as using as a lubricant for machinery and other uses where nutritional or health benefits are not required.

Refined coconut oil can also be used for cooking at extremely high temperatures, as the refining process means the oil is able to withstand a much higher heat. Check the brand's production practices to make sure they use natural steam and don't use chemical solvents.

There are a few preparations that use fractionated coconut oil for the benefits of its liquid state; for these, I recommend researching a good quality product.

The cost of coconut oil

When buying coconut oil you will generally find a big difference in price between refined and virgin and extra virgin oils and again with those that are organic, raw and cold or wet pressed. This usually reflects the extra time and labour involved in producing quality oil and it's worth buying the best you can afford.

Storage

Coconut oil is a stable oil, meaning it won't go rancid at room temperature. It's best stored in a cool, dark place, out of direct sunlight, in its original – preferably glass – container. If you live in a warm climate where the coconut oil is in its liquid state, you could refrigerate it to make it easier to use in its solid state. Although most products will give a 'best before' date on the jar, coconut oil won't go 'off' if stored correctly.

Introducing coconut oil to your diet

As with all potent foods it's important to gradually introduce coconut oil into your diet to ensure you don't experience any ill effects. Start with 1 teaspoon a day and gradually increase the amount. When using coconut oil on your body, do a patch test using a small amount first to ensure it's suitable for your skin.

Unless otherwise stated, all coconut oil used in the book is virgin/extra virgin.

Preparation

If you haven't cooked, cleaned, cleansed or moisturised with coconut oil before, you might be unfamiliar with how to prepare it before use.

Most of the preparations and recipes in this book require the oil to be in a softened or liquid state and there are various ways to do this, depending on the quantity and whether your oil is stored as a solid or liquid. For smaller amounts of solid coconut oil, the easiest way to soften it is to simply rub the solid oil gently between your fingertips until it reaches the correct consistency to be combined with other ingredients. With larger quantities, you will need to soften or melt the oil over heat.

Melting coconut oil

There are a number of melting methods that work well but my personal preference is the double boiler, as this retains the maximum health benefits of the oil. You'll see this in the preparation instructions in the book but if you prefer a different method, feel free to use it.

A double boiler is a gentle method of melting coconut oil and other ingredients: place a bowl over a pan filled with boiling water on the hob – take care that the water isn't too high in the pan and doesn't boil over. The solid oil is placed in the top bowl and heated gently until it melts. Alternatively, you can also place a bowl over another bowl that is filled with water from a boiled kettle – this will take longer to melt the ingredients.

You can also use a microwave to melt coconut oil, although take care to only power the microwave in short bursts until the oil is just melted and not too hot.

Storecupboard staples

Coconut oil can be used on its own for a number of health, beauty and household applications. However, when it's combined with other ingredients, its uses multiply significantly and you'll find that it becomes indispensable around the home. Below are some key ingredients that you might like to have to hand; these will enable you to create most of the preparations in the book. More unusual ingredients that are used less frequently are explained alongside the recipe or preparation that includes them.

Essential oils

Essential oils are the concentrated essence of various flowers and plants. They not only provide fragrance but also have a multitude of health benefits in their own right. The following oils are used in many preparations:
• Lavender
• Peppermint
• Rose
• Eucalyptus
• Frankincense

Shea butter

Shea butter is a fat that is extracted from the nut of the African shea tree. It's a great skin moisturiser and is used in several of the beauty preparations in this book. You should be able to find it online and in some health food shops. When buying, look for unrefined shea butter.

Cocoa butter

Cocoa butter is the fat of the cocoa bean. Like shea butter it has great moisturising properties but has a much more concentrated scent – of chocolate! Cocoa butter works well in body butters and creams, although the chocolate scent means that it is best combined with certain essential oils for fragrance. When buying, look for unrefined cocoa butter.

Aloe vera gel

Aloe vera gel is made from the inner part of the aloe vera leaf. It has a soothing and cooling effect on the skin and works extremely well when combined with coconut oil for various skin preparations. Look for organic and 100% aloe vera when buying.

Vitamin E oil

Vitamin E is an antioxidant so is excellent when combined with coconut oil in preparations for the skin. Some preparations only require a small amount so Vitamin E oil capsules are stated as the measurement, as they are readily available. However, you can also find larger packs of the oil in health food shops and online. Look for organic forms of vitamin E, such as wheat germ oil. As pure vitamin E is too sticky to package, check the ingredients list for added chemicals and fillers and choose a more natural and organic option.

Beeswax

Beeswax is produced by honey bees who use it to form the cells of their hives. It works well as a naturally hydrating ingredient and helps to bind and emulsify other ingredients. It's used in many of the salves and balms in this book. Look for good quality cosmetic-grade beeswax. Purchasing it in pellet or bead form will make it easier to measure and faster to melt than a solid bar of beeswax. You can find it online and in some health food stores.

Honey

Honey is an incredibly versatile ingredient with its own antibacterial properties. The honey used in most preparations and recipes in this book is regular runny honey. However, some recipes require the more solid form of set honey, in which case this is stated in the individual recipe. Choose the best quality honey you can afford, especially for preparations where it is being used on the skin.

Castile soap

Several centuries ago, all vegetable-based soaps were made in the Castile region of Spain, hence the name. Now, the name refers to any natural vegetable-based soap. Look for pure Castile to ensure you're getting a simple, ecological soap that is free from added chemical detergents.

Herbs and spices

I use various herbs and spices in the recipes and preparations in this book for their healing properties, taste and flavour. Try and keep a selection in the storecupboard, including cinnamon, ginger and turmeric.

Food

COCONUT OIL is naturally at home in the culinary world.
Having enjoyed a resurgence in popularity as a versatile
ingredient, coconut oil can be found in a wide range of
recipes, giving them all a dose of its metabolism-boosting
and blood sugar-balancing goodness.

As a staple oil, it's especially suited to cooking at higher
temperatures, as it won't become damaged in the same way
as other cooking oils: this makes it ideal for roasting and
frying, in particular.

Its natural, fresh flavour makes coconut oil particularly
well suited to cuisines such as Indian and Thai, as well as
an ideal ingredient in sweet, baked goods. Coconut oil's
solid state at room temperature also makes it the perfect
ingredient for holding together no-bake recipes, such
as snack bars, fudge, sweets and cheesecakes. It can also
be used as a replacement for butter in cooking and baking,
making recipes dairy free and vegan, if preferred.

Most of these recipes are free from refined sugar and use
wholegrain options where possible. Alternative sweetener
ideas are listed within the ingredients.

I'm confident that you'll find coconut oil a delicious and
versatile ingredient when cooking at home.

Breakfast

Often referred to as the most important meal of the day, there are plenty of ways to include coconut oil on your breakfast menu. Whether you're having a quick bowl of cereal before dashing out of the house, or you have time to enjoy a more leisurely meal, these recipes will energise you for the day ahead.

Blueberry and toasted coconut pancakes

Makes 4–6

225 g (8 oz) plain wholemeal flour
2½ tsp baking powder
1 tsp cinnamon
125 ml (4 fl oz) whole milk
125 ml (4 fl oz) plain yogurt
2 eggs
2 tbsp honey
2 tbsp coconut oil, plus extra for frying
225 g (8 oz) fresh or frozen blueberries, plus extra to serve
3 tbsp desiccated coconut
Maple syrup, to serve

Mix the flour, baking powder and cinnamon together in a bowl, leaving a well in the centre. In a separate bowl or jug, combine the milk, yogurt, eggs and honey. Melt the coconut oil and pour into the mixture, whisking constantly.

Add the liquid ingredients to the dry ingredients, mixing well until a smooth batter forms. Stir in the blueberries and let the batter rest.

Meanwhile, warm a pan over a medium heat and add the desiccated coconut, stirring constantly, until it becomes toasted and golden. Remove from the pan and set aside.

Place the pan back on the heat, adding 1 teaspoon of coconut oil. When the pan is hot and the coconut oil is melted, pour ¼ cup of the batter into the pan. Cook for 3–5 minutes, or until the underside is set and bubbles are starting to appear on the surface. Flip and cook the underside before removing from the pan and keeping warm on a plate in a low oven or under a low grill. Repeat with the remaining batter, adding more coconut oil to the pan before cooking each pancake.

Serve the pancakes topped with maple syrup, some fresh blueberries and a sprinkle of the toasted coconut.

Spiced pumpkin porridge

Serves 1

40 g (1½ oz) steel-cut porridge oats
150 ml (5 fl oz) water (or milk, if
    preferred)
60 g (2 oz) unsweetened canned
    pumpkin purée
1 tsp cinnamon
½ tsp ground ginger
1 tbsp coconut oil
1 tbsp maple syrup or honey
    (optional)
Ground cinnamon, to serve

Place the oats and water (or milk) in a pan over a medium heat. Leave to simmer and thicken, stirring at regular intervals, for 7–10 minutes.

Once thick and creamy, stir through the pumpkin purée, cinnamon, ginger, coconut oil and maple syrup or honey, if using. Serve with a sprinkle of ground cinnamon on top.

Raspberry and coconut porridge

Serves 1

2 tbsp desiccated coconut
40 g (1½ oz) steel-cut porridge oats
150 ml (5 fl oz) water (or milk, if
    preferred)
125 g (4 oz) fresh raspberries
1 tbsp coconut oil
1 tbsp maple syrup or honey
    (optional)

Add the desiccated coconut to a small pan over a medium high heat and toast, stirring often, for 2–3 minutes, until lightly golden. Set aside.

Place the oats and water (or milk) in a pan over a medium heat. Leave to simmer and thicken, stirring at regular intervals, for 7–10 minutes.

Once thick and creamy, stir through the raspberries, coconut oil and maple syrup or honey, if using. Serve with the toasted coconut on top.

Tips and ideas

Experiment with different additional ingredients with the basic porridge oats and water (or milk). Fresh berries, chopped nuts, and dried fruit are just some options that can be stirred into the basic recipe.

Cinnamon porridge

Serves 1

40 g (1½ oz) steel-cut porridge oats
150 ml (5 fl oz) water (or milk, if
   preferred)
1 tbsp coconut oil
1½ tsp cinnamon
1–2 tbsp maple syrup

For the topping:
1 tbsp coconut palm sugar or soft
   brown sugar
½ tsp cinnamon
1 tbsp coconut butter or manna

Place the oats and water (or milk) in a pan over a medium heat.
Leave to simmer and thicken, stirring at regular intervals, for
7–10 minutes.

Once thick and creamy, stir through the coconut oil, cinnamon and
maple syrup. Pour into a bowl and set aside while you prepare
the topping.

Mix the coconut sugar or brown sugar with the cinnamon and
sprinkle on top of the porridge, followed by a swirl of coconut butter
or manna (you may need to soften the coconut butter before using).

Apple, raisin and cinnamon porridge

Serves 1

40 g (1½ oz) steel-cut porridge oats
150 ml (5 fl oz) water (or milk, if
   preferred)
1 sweet eating apple
2 tbsp raisins
1 tsp cinnamon
1 tbsp coconut oil
1 tbsp maple syrup or honey
   (optional)
Ground cinnamon, to serve

Place the oats and water (or milk) in a pan over a medium heat. Chop
the apple into small pieces and add to the pan, along with the raisins
and cinnamon. Leave to simmer and thicken, stirring at regular
intervals, for 7–10 minutes.

Once thick and creamy, stir through the coconut oil and maple syrup
or honey, if using. Serve with a sprinkle of cinnamon.

Banana nut porridge

Serves 1

40 g (1½ oz) steel-cut porridge oats
150 ml (5 fl oz) water (or milk, if
   preferred)
1 banana
1 tbsp coconut oil
1 tbsp maple syrup or honey
   (optional)
25 g (1 oz) walnuts

Place the oats and water (or milk) in a pan over a medium heat. Leave
to simmer and thicken, stirring at regular intervals, for 7–10 minutes.

Mash the banana well and add to the pan, mixing well to combine.
Add the coconut oil and maple syrup or honey, if using. Roughly
chop the walnuts and scatter over the porridge before serving.

Chai spice and almond granola

Makes 6–8 servings

150 g (5 oz) almonds
150 g (5 oz) cashew nuts
175 g (6 oz) jumbo oats
Pinch of sea salt
1 tsp cinnamon
½ tsp ground ginger
¼ tsp ground cloves
2 tbsp coconut oil
75 ml (2½ fl oz) honey
60 g (2 oz) almond butter

Preheat the oven to 175°C (350°F). Roughly chop the almonds and cashews and combine with the oats, salt and spices in a large bowl.

Melt the coconut oil in a double boiler and mix with the honey and almond butter. Pour the coconut oil mix on top of the oats and nuts and stir well to coat evenly.

Line a baking tray with greaseproof paper. Spread the granola over the baking tray in a single layer (use more baking trays if needed). Bake for 10–20 minutes, turning the granola often to ensure even cooking. Remove from the oven when golden brown and toasted.

Leave to cool then store in an airtight container for up to 2 weeks.

Chocolate hazelnut granola

Makes 6–8 servings

150 g (5 oz) cashew nuts
175 g (6 oz) jumbo oats
75 g (2½ oz) pumpkin seeds
75 g (2½ oz) sunflower seeds
60 g (2 oz) coconut oil
75 ml (2½ fl oz) honey
25 g (1 oz) cocoa powder
½ tsp salt

Preheat the oven to 175°C (350°F). Roughly chop the hazelnuts and combine with the oats and seeds in a large bowl.

Melt the coconut oil in a double boiler and mix with the honey, cocoa powder and salt. Pour the coconut oil mix on top of the oats and nuts and stir well to coat evenly.

Line a baking tray with greaseproof paper. Spread the granola over the baking tray in a single layer (use more baking trays, if needed). Bake for 10–20 minutes, turning the granola often to ensure even cooking. Remove from the oven when golden brown and toasted.

Leave to cool then store in an airtight container for up to 2 weeks.

Coconut, vanilla and almond granola

Makes 6–8 servings

150 g (5 oz) almonds
175 g (6 oz) jumbo oats
100 g (3½ oz) desiccated coconut
Pinch of sea salt
2 tbsp coconut oil
75 ml (2½ fl oz) honey
60 g (2 oz) almond butter
2 tsp vanilla extract

Preheat the oven to 175°C (350°F). Roughly chop the almonds and combine with the oats, desiccated coconut and salt in a large bowl.

Melt the coconut oil in a double boiler and mix with the honey, almond butter and vanilla extract. Pour the coconut oil mix on top of the oats and nuts and stir well to coat evenly.

Line a baking tray with greaseproof paper. Spread the granola over the baking tray in a single layer (use more baking trays, if needed). Bake for 10–20 minutes, turning the granola often to ensure even cooking. Remove from the oven when golden brown and toasted.

Leave to cool then store in an airtight container for up to 2 weeks.

Drinks

Smoothies make perfect on-the-go breakfasts. They're quick and easy to blend and packed with the goodness of fruit (and sometimes vegetables). However, they aren't always filling and that's where coconut oil works as a super addition. As well as offering nutritional benefits, the oil makes smoothies more filling, leading to more stable energy levels. Make sure you blend the smoothie well to remove any coconut oil lumps.

Tropical blast smoothie

Serves 1

225 g (8 oz) fresh pineapple chunks
100 g (3½ oz) mango (fresh
    or frozen)
1 tbsp coconut oil
1 cup coconut water

Add all the ingredients to a blender and blend well until smooth. Pour into a tall glass and enjoy.

Super creamy green smoothie

Serves 1

25 g (1 oz) spinach
1 ripe banana
½ avocado
1 tbsp coconut oil
225 ml (8 fl oz) water or milk

Add all the ingredients to a blender and blend well until smooth. Pour into a tall glass and enjoy.

Detoxifying green smoothie

Serves 1

25 g (1 oz) spinach
1 ripe banana
7.5-cm (3-in) piece cucumber, cut
    into chunks
1 tbsp coconut oil
225 ml (8 fl oz) water or milk
2–4 ice cubes (optional)

Add all the ingredients to a blender and blend well until smooth. Pour into a tall glass and enjoy.

Strawberries and cream smoothie

Serves 1

225 g (8 oz) fresh strawberries
1 banana
225 ml (8 fl oz) Greek-style yogurt
    (or coconut yogurt for dairy-free)
1 tbsp coconut oil
225 ml (8 fl oz) full-fat milk (or
    non-dairy milk)
2–4 ice cubes (optional)

Add all the ingredients to a blender and blend well until smooth. Pour into a tall glass and enjoy.

Chocolate cherry smoothie

Serves 1

100 g (3½ oz) frozen cherries
1 ripe banana
1 tbsp cocoa powder
1 tbsp coconut oil
225 ml (8 fl oz) water

Add all the ingredients to a blender and blend well until smooth. Pour into a tall glass and enjoy.

Blueberry and coconut smoothie

Serves 1

225 g (8 oz) blueberries (fresh or frozen)
100 g (3½ oz) chopped mango
1 tbsp coconut oil
225 ml (8 fl oz) water (or milk)
2 tbsp canned coconut milk

Add the blueberries, mango, coconut oil and water (or milk) to a blender and blend until smooth.

Pour into a tall glass and top with canned coconut milk.

Warm pear and ginger cold-fighting smoothie

Serves 1

1 large pear, peeled, cored and cut into chunks
225 ml (8 fl oz) non-dairy milk
1 tsp ground ginger
½ tsp cinnamon
1 tbsp coconut oil

Place the pear in a steamer basket and steam for 5–10 minutes, until soft.

In a separate pan, warm the non-dairy milk.

Add the steamed pear, warmed milk, spices and coconut oil to a blender and blend until smooth.

Serve warm in a glass or mug.

Coconut oil coffee

Serves 1

**225 ml (8 fl oz) good-quality brewed
   coffee**
½–1 tbsp coconut oil

Add the coconut oil to the
coffee. Alternatively, blend in a
blender or using a whisk, until
the coffee becomes foamy.

Dressings and dips

From light lunches to picnics, parties and snacks, it's good to have a range of easy-to-prepare salad dressings and dips that you can whisk up at a moment's notice. Here, coconut oil gives homemade mayonnaise a makeover, while it also adds another flavour dimension to dips.

Mayonnaise

Makes 350 ml (12 fl oz)

1 egg, plus 2 egg yolks
1 tbsp Dijon mustard
Juice from ½ lemon
½ tsp salt
100 g (3½ oz) coconut oil
125 ml (4½ fl oz) extra virgin
    olive oil

Add the egg, egg yolks, mustard, lemon juice and salt to a food processor or blender and blend to combine. Melt the coconut oil in a double boiler until it's just melted (not too hot). With the food processor or blender running on low, drizzle in the olive oil and coconut oil.

Transfer to a jar and keep refrigerated. The mayonnaise will keep for up to 1 week.

Coconut oil salad dressing

Makes 350 ml (12 fl oz)

75 g (2½ oz) coconut oil
75 ml (2½ fl oz) olive oil
75 ml (2½ fl oz) apple cider vinegar
1 tbsp honey
1 clove garlic, finely chopped
½ tsp dried Italian seasoning
Generous pinch of salt
Freshly ground black pepper,
    to taste

Melt the coconut oil in a double boiler and set aside. Place the remaining ingredients in a bowl and whisk well. Continue whisking while you drizzle in the liquid coconut oil.

Transfer to a glass jar or bottle and store in the refrigerator. Return to room temperature and shake well before adding to your salad.

The salad dressing will keep for up to 2 weeks in the fridge.

Warm peanut butter coconut dip

Makes 225 ml (8 fl oz)

100 g (3½ oz) coconut oil
125 g (4½ oz) smooth peanut butter
1–2 tbsp honey (for a sweet dip)
½ tsp finely chopped red chilli and
    ½ tbsp soy sauce (for a spicy dip)
Salt to taste

Melt the coconut oil in a double boiler. Add the peanut butter while the coconut oil is still warm in the double boiler. Stir well to combine, adding any of the sweet or savoury additions.

Transfer to a bowl and serve immediately, or transfer to a jar and store in the fridge, warming in a bowl of warm water before use.

Spicy avocado dip

Makes 225 ml (8 fl oz)

2 ripe avocados
Juice of 1 lime
1 clove garlic, crushed
½ tsp salt
2 tbsp coconut oil
2 tbsp water
1 red chilli, finely chopped
1 small red onion, finely chopped
25 g (1 oz) fresh coriander, finely
    chopped

Scoop the flesh out of the avocados and add to a food processor or blender with the lime juice, garlic and salt. Melt the coconut oil in a double boiler and set aside.

Blend the avocado until smooth, scraping down the sides, if needed. With the food processor running, drizzle in the coconut oil, blending until well incorporated. Add the water, 1 tablespoon at a time (if needed), to loosen the consistency. Transfer the dip to a bowl and set aside.

Gently fold the chilli, onion and coriander into the dip. Transfer to a bowl (if serving immediately) or an airtight container. The dip will keep in the fridge for up to 3 days.

Curried hummus

Makes 350 ml (12 fl oz)

1 x 400 g (14 oz) can chickpeas
1 clove garlic, crushed
4 tbsp tahini sesame paste
Juice from 1 lemon
½ tsp mild curry powder, plus
    extra to serve
½ tsp ground cumin
Large pinch turmeric
¼ tsp salt
2–6 tbsp water (as needed)
2 tbsp coconut oil

Drain the chickpeas, rinse and place in a blender or food processor. Add the garlic to the processor with the tahini, lemon juice, curry powder, cumin, turmeric and salt. Blend until thickened and smooth, adding 1 tablespoon of water at a time to loosen the texture, if needed.

Melt the coconut oil in a warm place. With the food processor running, drizzle in the coconut oil, plus more water, as needed (the hummus will firm up once chilled, so add enough water to keep the consistency loose).

Transfer to a bowl or jar and serve with a sprinkle of curry powder.

Tips and ideas

Adding coconut oil to this curried hummus results in a firmer texture. It also complements the richness of the spices.

Curries

Coconut oil is an excellent addition to curries, providing richness and a delicious subtle coconut flavour. It also balances out the heat of fiery dishes, adding a freshness that complements herbs such as coriander.

Coconut vegetable curry

Serves 4

3 tbsp coconut oil
1 aubergine, cubed
1 onion, finely chopped
2 tbsp mild curry powder
1 tsp ground cumin
½ tsp ground coriander
2 medium sweet potatoes, cubed
1 x 400 g (14 oz) can coconut milk
2 x 400 g (14 oz) cans green lentils
1 red or yellow pepper, sliced
Brown or white rice, to serve
Chopped fresh coriander, to serve

Add 1 tablespoon of coconut oil to a large pan or wok over a medium-high heat. Add the aubergine and fry until lightly browned all over. Remove from the pan and set aside.

Add the remaining coconut oil to the pan. Add the onion, curry powder, ground cumin and ground coriander and fry for 3–5 minutes, until the spices are fragrant and the onion has turned translucent.

Add the sweet potatoes and coconut milk and bring to a low simmer for 20 minutes, or until the sweet potato is beginning to soften.

Drain the lentils and add to the pan with the aubergine and pepper. Continue to cook until the sweet potatoes are completely tender and the pepper has softened.

Serve with brown or white rice and chopped fresh coriander.

Thai green chicken curry

Serves 4

For the curry paste:
4 cloves garlic, crushed
½ onion, chopped
2 lemon grass stalks, peeled and chopped
5-cm (2-in) piece fresh ginger, peeled and chopped
4 green chillies
1 tsp ground cumin
60 g (2 oz) fresh coriander
2 tbsp fish sauce
1 tbsp coconut oil

For the curry:
2 tbsp coconut oil
450 g (1 lb) skinless, boneless chicken thigh fillets, diced
2 x 400 g (14 oz) cans coconut milk
1 red pepper, finely sliced
225 g (8 oz) mangetout
Brown or white rice, to serve
Chopped fresh coriander, to serve
2 limes, cut into wedges, to serve

To make the curry paste, add all the ingredients to a food processor and process until a thick paste forms.

In a large pan or wok, warm the coconut oil over a medium heat. Add 4 heaped tablespoons of the curry paste (keep any leftover paste in the fridge) and gently fry for 5 minutes, until fragrant.

Add the diced chicken and fry for 1–2 minutes, then add the coconut milk and increase the heat until it is simmering. Simmer for 20 minutes, until the chicken is cooked and tender.

Add the pepper and mangetout and simmer for a further 5 minutes.

Serve with brown or white rice, a scattering of fresh coriander and lime wedges.

Chickpea and butternut korma

Serves 4

1 tbsp coconut oil
1 medium butternut squash,
   peeled and cubed
2 x 400 g (14 oz) cans chickpeas
Brown or white rice, or naan
   bread, to serve
Chopped fresh coriander, to
   serve

For the korma sauce:
60 g (2 oz) coconut oil
60 g (2 oz) cashew pieces
225 ml (8 fl oz) vegetable stock,
   plus extra, if needed
225 ml (8 fl oz) Greek yogurt
60 g (2 oz) tomato concentrate
1 tbsp honey
3 tsp garam masala
1 tsp cinnamon
1 tsp turmeric
1 tsp ground coriander
½ tsp cumin

This creamy korma can also be made with chicken – in place of, or as well as, the chickpeas. You will have extra sauce, so keep half in the fridge or freeze it for another time.

Preheat the oven to 200°C (400°F).

Melt the coconut oil in a double boiler. Toss the butternut squash with the coconut oil and place in a single layer on a baking tray. Bake for 30–40 minutes until tender. Set aside.

While the squash is roasting, purée all the sauce ingredients in a food processor and set aside.

Drain and rinse the chickpeas and add to a large pan, along with the butternut squash. Add around half of the korma sauce and bring to a simmer, adding further vegetable stock to thin the sauce, if required. Simmer until heated through and serve with rice or naan and chopped coriander.

Lentil dhal

Serves 2–4

400 g (14 oz) red lentils
2 tbsp coconut oil
1 onion, finely chopped
2 cloves garlic, crushed
5-cm (2-in) piece fresh ginger,
    peeled and grated
1 tsp turmeric
½ tsp salt
475 ml (16 fl oz) vegetable stock
1 tsp. garam masala
100 ml (3½ fl oz) coconut milk
Rice or naan, to serve
Chopped fresh parsley, to serve

This lentil dhal includes two anti-inflammatory super foods: coconut oil and turmeric. It can be served with rice or naan as a main meal, or simply on its own, similar to a thick soup.

Pick over and rinse the lentils in a sieve. In a large pan, warm the coconut oil over a medium heat. Add the onion, garlic, ginger, turmeric and salt and fry gently for 2 minutes, stirring constantly.

Add the lentils and vegetable stock and bring the pan to a simmer. Cover and cook for 15 minutes. Add the garam masala and coconut milk and stir well. Continue to simmer until the dhal is thick.

Serve with rice or naan and chopped parsley.

Roast meat and vegetables

Coconut oil works beautifully with roast chicken, creating a crispy skin and moist meat, while also adding extra flavour to the dish. If you're entertaining more than four people, cook a large chicken and adjust the cooking times accordingly. You will also need to increase the amount of coconut oil for the paste, depending on the size of the chicken.

Lemon, garlic and rosemary roast chicken

Serves 4

1 medium chicken
75 g (2½ oz) coconut oil
2 lemons
6 cloves garlic (2 finely chopped)
2 sprigs fresh rosemary

Preheat the oven to 190°C (375°F). Remove any giblets from the chicken cavity and place in a large roasting tray. Cover and leave to reach room temperature.

Soften the coconut oil in a double boiler. Zest the lemons. Combine the lemon zest, chopped garlic and coconut oil into a paste.

Cut the lemons in half and place inside the cavity of the chicken with the 4 whole garlic cloves and 1 sprig of rosemary, snapped into pieces, if needed. Rub the coconut oil mix over the chicken, pushing some under the skin, on top of the breasts. Thread the remaining sprig of rosemary through the gap between the chicken legs.

Place in the oven and roast according to instructions (usually 20 minutes per 450 g/ 1 lb, plus 20 minutes). Check every 30 minutes, basting the chicken with the juices that collect in the bottom of the roasting tray. Check the chicken is cooked through using a probe thermometer or by piercing the flesh above the thigh and checking that the juices run clear.

Leave to rest for 15 minutes then carve the chicken and serve.

Variations

Sweet chilli and lime roast chicken: replace the lemons with 1 lime, use 1 garlic clove and replace the rosemary with 2 finely chopped red chillies and 2 tablespoons of honey. Rub the mix over the chicken and follow the recipe as before.

Chinese 5 spice roasted chicken: use 1 garlic clove and replace the lemons and rosemary with 3 tablespoons of Chinese 5 spice powder, 2 tablespoons of honey and 1 tablespoon of soy sauce. Rub the mix over the chicken and follow the recipe as before.

Roasted sweet potatoes

1 medium sweet potato
  per person
½–1 tbsp coconut oil
  per person
Salt and freshly ground black
  pepper

Preheat the oven to 190°C (375°F).

To roast whole, rub the sweet potatoes in coconut oil and salt and wrap in kitchen foil. Cook the sweet potatoes until tender – about 1 hour, depending on size.

To roast in wedges, rounds or cubes, chop the sweet potatoes into even-sized pieces. Place on a roasting tray and add the coconut oil. Place in the oven for 5 minutes, remove the tray and toss the sweet potato in the melted oil to coat all over. Return to the oven and bake until tender, about 30–40 minutes.

Season with salt and pepper to taste and serve.

Mediterranean vegetables

Serves 4

2 large peppers, cubed
1 small aubergine, cubed
1 courgette, cubed
2 red onions, cut into wedges
2 tbsp coconut oil
Salt and freshly ground black
  pepper

Preheat the oven to 190°C (375°F). Place the vegetables on a baking tray with the coconut oil. Roast in the oven for 5 minutes then take out and toss the vegetables in the melted oil.

Return to the oven and bake until softened and golden around the edges, about 30–40 minutes.

Season with salt and pepper to taste and serve.

Roasted root vegetables

Serves 4

1 small butternut squash,
  deseeded and cut into wedges
1 parsnip, cubed
1 small swede, cubed
2 tbsp coconut oil
Salt and freshly ground black
  pepper

Preheat the oven to 190°C (375°F). Place the vegetables onto 1 or 2 baking trays and add the coconut oil. Place in the oven for 5 minutes then take out and toss the vegetables in the melted oil.

Return to the oven and bake until softened, about 30–40 minutes.

Season with salt and pepper to taste and serve.

Kale chips

Serves 4

6–8 large stems kale
2 tbsp coconut oil
½ tsp salt

Preheat the oven to 130°C (275°F). Strip the kale leaves from the tough stems, discarding the stems. Tear the leaves into bite-sized pieces. Wash the leaves and dry thoroughly (any dampness will make the kale chips soggy).

Line 2 or 3 baking trays with greaseproof paper. Lay the kale out in a single layer over the sheets.

Melt the coconut oil in a double boiler and drizzle over the kale. Massage into all of the leaves and sprinkle over the salt.

Bake in the oven for about 20 minutes, checking every 5 minutes, until the kale is crispy. Leave to cool before serving.

Roast fruit

You may not have tried roasting fruit before but trust me when I say it's worth it. Roasting intensifies the sweetness and slightly caramelises the fruit. It works well with both sweet and savoury dishes – try it with ice cream or yogurt for a simple dessert, or serve with roast meat or as a pizza topping.

Roast peaches and nectarines

Serves 4

900 g (2 lb) mixed peaches and nectarines
2 tbsp coconut oil

Preheat the oven to 200°C (400°F). Wash and dry the fruit. Slice in half, remove the stones then slice in half again so you have quarters.

Melt the coconut oil in a double boiler, place the fruit on a baking tray and pour over the oil. Toss the fruit pieces in the oil so they are evenly coated.

Bake for 15–20 minutes, or until the fruit is soft, tender and starting to turn golden at the edges.

Roast plums with almonds

Serves 2

450 g (1 lb) plums
1 tbsp coconut oil
2 tbsp flaked almonds
Ice cream or custard, to serve

Preheat the oven to 200°C (400°F). Wash and dry the plums. Slice in half, remove the stones then slice in half again so you have quarters.

Melt the coconut oil in a double boiler, place the plums on a baking tray and pour over the oil. Toss the plum quarters in the oil so they are evenly coated.

Bake for 10–15 minutes or until the fruit is soft, tender and starting to turn golden at the edges.

Scatter over the flaked almonds and return to the oven. Increase the temperature to 220°C (430°F) and roast for a further 5 minutes. Serve with ice cream or custard.

Tips and ideas

Roasting is a handy way to use up fruit that hasn't ripened well, as it will soften during cooking.

Snacks: popcorn, bars and bites

Try these quick and easy snacks for lunch boxes, coffee breaks and teatime treats. As well as coconut oil, many of the recipes have other healthy ingredients packed inside.

Peanut butter chocolate chip energy bites

Makes 8–10

125 g (4½ oz) rolled oats
60 g (2 oz) chocolate chips
2 tbsp chia seeds (optional)
Generous pinch of salt
60 g (2 oz) coconut oil
75 g (2½ oz) crunchy peanut
   butter
75 ml (2½ fl oz) honey

Combine the oats, chocolate chips, chia seeds (if using) and salt in a large bowl.

Melt the coconut oil in a double boiler (until just melted – not hot or the chocolate chips will melt) and combine with the peanut butter and honey.

Pour over the oat mixture and stir well to combine. Roll the mixture into small balls and place on a plate or tray. Refrigerate until firm. Store in an airtight container in the fridge for up to 1 week.

Popcorn

Serves 4

3 tbsp coconut oil
75 g (2½ oz) popcorn kernels
Salt or sugar, to sprinkle

Place the coconut oil in the bottom of a large pan with a lid and melt over a medium-high heat. Add 3–4 popcorn kernels, cover the pan and wait for them to pop.

When they pop add the rest of the kernels and take the pan off the heat, just for a few seconds. This helps all the kernels to pop at the same time and avoids any burning.

Return the pan to the heat, covered but with a small gap to let steam escape, and wait for the kernels to pop. When the popping slows down, give the pan a shake then tip the popcorn into a large bowl. Sprinkle with salt or sugar. Leave to cool and serve.

Tips and ideas

For a variation on standard popcorn, try adding a little chile powder instead of salt or sugar.

Raw snack balls

Makes 8–10

150 g (5 oz) almonds (or other nuts such as cashews, walnut or hazelnuts)
175 g (6 oz) dried dates
2 tbsp coconut oil
¼ tsp salt

Using completely raw ingredients means that all the beneficial enzymes are still intact. This simple recipe is super versatile – try adding other ingredients, such as cocoa powder, for new flavours.

Place the almonds in a food processor and process until finely chopped. Add the dates, coconut oil and salt and process until the mixture comes together.

Remove from the processor and roll pieces of the mixture into balls. Store in an airtight container in the fridge for up to 1 week.

Oatmeal and raisin flapjacks

Makes 9

175 g (6 oz) rolled oats
150 g (5 oz) raisins
1 tsp. ground cinnamon
4 tbsp coconut oil, plus extra for greasing
175 ml (6 fl oz) unsweetened apple sauce
175 ml (6 fl oz) maple syrup or honey

Preheat the oven to 175°C (350°F). Combine the oats, raisins and cinnamon in a large bowl.

Melt the coconut oil in a double boiler. Add the apple sauce and maple syrup to the coconut oil and stir to combine. Pour into the dry ingredients and mix well.

Grease a 20 x 20-cm (8 x 8-in) baking tray with coconut oil and pour in the mix, patting it down firmly with the back of a spoon.

Bake for 20–25 minutes until golden brown. Leave to cool in the tin before removing and cutting into slices.

No-bake granola bars

Makes 6

75 g (2½ oz) coconut oil, plus extra for greasing
175 g (6 oz) porridge oats
75 g (2½ oz) almond butter
75 g (2½ oz) chopped almonds
25 g (1 oz) pumpkin seeds
25 g (1 oz) sunflower seeds
75 ml (2½ fl oz) honey
1 tsp vanilla extract
½ tsp cinnamon
¼ tsp salt

These no-bake granola bars are easy to make and the mixture is held together by the coconut oil and almond butter. They're packed with nutrient-dense nuts and seeds to make the perfect snack or breakfast on the go.

Melt the coconut oil in a double boiler and combine with the rest of the ingredients in a large bowl.

Grease a 20 x 20-cm (8 x 8-in.) baking tray with coconut oil and pour in the mix, patting it down firmly with the back of a spoon.

Refrigerate or freeze until firm. Remove from the tin and slice into 6 bars. Store the bars wrapped in kitchen foil in the fridge for up to 1 week, or the freezer for up to 6 months.

Snacks: roasted nuts and seeds

Nuts and seeds make a delicious and healthy snack. Roast them with coconut oil and some extra ingredients to create a range of flavours.

Honey-roasted nuts and seeds

Serves 4 as a snack

150 g (5 oz) almonds
75 g (2½ oz) cashews
25 g (1 oz) pumpkin seeds
25 g (1 oz) sunflower seeds
3 tbsp coconut palm sugar or soft
   brown sugar
½ tsp cinnamon
½ tsp salt
2 tbsp water
3 tbsp honey
2 tsp coconut oil

Preheat the oven to 175°C (350°F). Line a baking tray with greaseproof paper and add the nuts and seeds. Roast for 10 minutes until golden brown then set aside to cool.

In a small bowl combine the sugar, cinnamon and salt. Add the water, honey and coconut oil to a pan and bring to a boil over a medium-high heat, stirring constantly.

Add the nuts and seeds to the pan, stirring constantly so they become coated in the honey mixture. Add 2 tablespoons of the sugar mixture and continue to stir the nuts until caramelised on the outside.

Transfer to a large bowl, add the rest of the sugar mixture and mix well. Lay the nuts and seeds out on a sheet of baking paper and leave to cool and harden.

Store in an airtight container for up to 2 weeks.

Spicy roasted cashews

Serves 4 as a snack

300 g (10 oz) cashew nuts
1 tsp hot chilli powder
½ tsp salt
2 tbsp coconut oil

Preheat the oven to 160°C (325°F). Place the cashews in a bowl with the chilli powder and salt. Melt the coconut oil in a double boiler and pour over the cashews, mixing well to coat them in the oil.

Pour onto a lined baking tray. Roast for 10–15 minutes, mixing regularly to ensure they roast evenly and don't burn.

Leave to cool and store in an airtight container for up to 2 weeks.

Tamari-toasted seeds

Serves 4 as a snack

1 tbsp coconut oil
150 g (5 oz) pumpkin seeds
150 g (5 oz) sunflower seeds
2–3 tbsp tamari or soy sauce

Place ½ tablespoon of the coconut oil in a frying pan over a medium-high heat. Add 75 g (2 ½ oz) of the pumpkin seeds and 75 g (2 ½ oz) of the sunflower seeds to the pan, along with half of the tamari or soy sauce and toast the seeds, stirring constantly.

Once the seeds are golden and starting to pop, remove from the pan and leave to cool. Repeat with the remaining seeds.

Store in an airtight container for up to 2 weeks.

Sweet cinnamon-roasted almonds

Serves 4 as a snack

300 g (10 oz) almonds
60 g (2 oz) coconut palm sugar or
    soft brown sugar
2 tsp cinnamon
½ tsp salt
2 tbsp coconut oil

Preheat the oven to 160°C (325°F). Place the almonds in a bowl with the coconut palm sugar, cinnamon and salt. Melt the coconut oil in a double boiler and pour over the almonds, mixing well to coat them in the oil and sugar.

Pour the almonds onto a lined baking tray. Roast for 15–20 minutes, mixing regularly to ensure they roast and caramelise evenly.

Leave to cool and store in an airtight container for up to 2 weeks.

Tips and ideas

Feel free to add some dried fruit or chocolate chips to the sweet recipes to create a variation for a selection of different snack mixes.

Snacks: spreads

Try these spreads on toast or as a dip for fruit. They combine all the goodness of coconut oil with some delicious additions.

Chocolate hazelnut spread

Makes 450 g (1 lb)

300 g (10 oz) hazelnuts
   (or 300g/10 oz) readymade
   hazelnut butter)
60 g (2 oz) dark chocolate chips
1 tbsp coconut oil
1 tbsp honey
2 tbsp cocoa powder
1 tsp sea salt

Preheat the oven to 160°C (325°F). Place the hazelnuts on a baking tray and roast for 10 minutes until they start to turn golden. Leave to cool for 5–10 minutes, then lay on a clean kitchen towel. Fold the towel over and rub the hazelnuts so the skins come off.

Remove the hazelnuts from the towel and place in a food processor. Process for 10–20 minutes (stopping regularly to give your food processor a break) until they become hazelnut butter with a liquid-like texture.

Melt the chocolate chips, coconut oil and honey in a double boiler until liquid. Add the cocoa powder and salt.

With the food processor on, drizzle the chocolate mixture into the hazelnut butter until completely incorporated.

Transfer to a jar and store in the fridge. Let the spread come to room temperature, or warm before using.

Chocolate spread

Makes 300 g (10 oz)

1 x 400 g (14 oz) can coconut milk
60 g (2 oz) coconut oil
75 ml (2½ fl oz) honey
25 g (1 oz) cocoa powder

Place the can of coconut milk in the fridge to chill. Melt the coconut oil in a double boiler and combine with the honey and cocoa powder.

Remove the coconut milk from the fridge and, without shaking the can, open it and scoop out the solid coconut cream that has accumulated at the top. Mix with the rest of the ingredients.

Transfer to a small jar and store in the fridge. If liked, you can soften the spread by placing the jar in a bowl of warm water before using.

Strawberry spread

You can make a banana version of this spread by substituting the strawberries and honey with 2 ripe bananas, 125 g (4 ½ oz) peanut butter and ½ teaspoon salt.

Makes 1 cup

100 g (3½ oz) coconut oil
350 g (12 oz) strawberries
75 ml (2½ fl oz) honey

Melt the coconut oil in a double boiler and add to a food processor or blender, along with the rest of the ingredients. Blend until smooth.

Transfer to a small jar and store in the fridge. If liked, you can soften the spread by placing the jar in a bowl of warm water before using.

Chocolate

Coconut oil works really well with chocolate-based recipes and it adds another dimension to the flavour of the finished recipe. Try this selection of sweets, desserts and cakes for an instant cocoa hit.

Brownies

Makes 9

6 tbsp coconut oil
175 g (6 oz) dark chocolate chips
150 g (5 oz) coconut palm sugar or
    granulated sugar
2 large eggs
2 tsp vanilla extract
25 g (1 oz) cocoa powder
3 tbsp cornflour
¼ tsp salt
75 g (2½ oz) walnuts (optional)

Brownies are the ultimate chocolate dessert. This recipe is gluten free and can also be dairy free if you use dairy-free chocolate chips.

Preheat the oven to 175°C (350°F). Line a 20 x 20-cm (8 x 8-in) baking tray with greaseproof paper.

Melt the coconut oil and chocolate chips in a double boiler and set aside.

Beat the sugar, eggs, and vanilla, using an electric hand whisk or stand mixer, until smooth and fluffy. Add the melted chocolate and coconut oil and mix until well combined. Add the cocoa powder, cornflour and salt and whisk again until you have a thick, smooth batter. Roughly chop the walnuts, if using, and fold into the batter.

Pour the batter into the baking pan and smooth the surface with the back of a spoon. Bake for 25 minutes until the surface is set.

Leave to cool for 20 minutes before removing from the pan. Cut into 9 squares and serve warm or store in an airtight container for up to 5 days. The brownies can also be wrapped in foil and frozen.

Coconut oil chocolates

Makes 10–12

100 g (3½ oz) coconut oil
60 g (2 oz) cocoa powder
2–3 tbsp honey
Generous pinch of salt

Try adding mint or orange flavouring, chopped nuts or dried fruit to create new flavours and textures.

Melt the coconut oil in a double boiler and combine with the cocoa powder, honey and salt.

Pour into silicone moulds and leave to harden in the fridge (or freezer, if you're impatient!). Pop out of the moulds and store in an airtight container in the fridge.

Chocolate mousse

This rich and indulgent chocolate mousse is free from dairy and refined sugar and packed with healthy fats.

Serves 4

3 tbsp coconut oil
2 large ripe avocados
100 ml (3½ fl oz) honey (or other liquid sweetener)
60 g (2 oz) cocoa powder, plus extra for dusting
¼ tsp salt

Melt the coconut oil in a double boiler. Place all the other ingredients into a food processor or blender and blend until smooth and well incorporated, stopping to scrape down the sides, if needed.

With the motor running on a low speed, drizzle in the coconut oil until incorporated.

Divide the mousse between 4 pots or cups and refrigerate until required. Serve with a dusting of cocoa powder.

Chocolate magic shell for ice cream

Add a crisp chocolate coating to your ice cream desserts with this indulgent magic shell that hardens as it cools.

Serves 4

60 g (2 oz) dark chocolate chips
75 g (2½ oz) coconut oil

Melt the chocolate and coconut oil together in a double boiler.

Use immediately, or transfer to a jar to store at room temperature. To use again, warm up by placing the jar in a bowl of warm water until liquid, then pour over the dessert for it to set.

Pistachio, goji and coconut chocolate bark

Crunchy and crisp chocolate bark makes a beautiful gift or indulgent treat. Decorated with tasty nuts and dried fruit, try this version and then experiment with other toppings to create your own.

100 g (3½ oz) coconut oil
60 g (2 oz) cocoa powder
2 tbsp honey
¼ tsp salt
40 g (1½ oz) pistachios
60 g (2 oz) goji berries
25 g (1 oz) desiccated coconut

Melt the coconut oil in a double boiler. Combine with the cocoa powder, honey and salt.

Line a baking tray with greaseproof paper. Pour the chocolate into the baking sheet and let it spread out to fill the tray.

Roughly chop the pistachios and scatter on top of the chocolate, followed by the goji berries and desiccated coconut. Press down any pieces of the nuts and goji berries that haven't stuck to the chocolate base.

Place the baking tray in the fridge or freezer and leave to harden completely. Break into large pieces and store in an airtight container in the fridge.

Chocolate fondue

Perfect as a sweet dip for fruit or marshmallows, try this chocolate fondue for your next party.

Serves 4

100 g (3½ oz) dark chocolate chips
100 g (3½ oz) coconut oil
2 tbsp honey

Melt all the ingredients together in a double boiler until liquid. Transfer to a bowl and serve immediately.

Cakes and pastries

Coconut oil is a wonderful ingredient in baked recipes. It can be used to replace butter to create dairy-free versions of your favourite treats.

Coconut and banana chocolate chip bread

Serves 8–10

60 g (2 oz) coconut flour
60 g (2 oz) ground almonds
¾ tsp bicarbonate of soda
25 g (1 oz) desiccated coconut
2–3 bananas
4 eggs (at room temperature)
100 ml (3½ fl oz) honey or maple syrup
100 g (3½ oz) coconut oil, plus extra for greasing
60 g (2 oz) dark chocolate chips

Preheat the oven to 175°C (350°F). Line a standard loaf tin with greaseproof paper and grease the inside with coconut oil.

Combine the coconut flour, ground almonds, bicarbonate of soda and desiccated coconut in a large bowl. Mash the bananas and combine with the eggs and honey. Stir into the dry ingredients.

Melt the coconut oil in a double boiler and pour into the bowl in a thin stream, stirring constantly. Fold in the chocolate chips. Transfer the batter to the loaf tin (the batter will be very thick) and smooth the surface.

Bake for 50 minutes then cover the top with foil to prevent over-browning. Bake for a further 15–20 minutes until a skewer inserted into the middle of the loaf comes out clean.

Leave to cool for 15 minutes before removing from the tin and cooling on a rack. The loaf will keep in an airtight container for 5 days or slices can be wrapped in kitchen foil and frozen for up to 6 months.

Tips and ideas

This delicious moist banana bread is gluten free and can also be dairy free if made with dairy-free chocolate chips. It uses coconut flour, another incredible coconut product that is full of fibre and naturally lower in carbohydrates, which works well in coconut oil recipes as it is highly absorbent. You should be able to find it at your local health food shop or online.

Coconut cake

Serves 8

100 g (3½ oz) coconut oil
125 ml (4½ fl oz) coconut cream
75 g (2½ oz) coconut palm sugar or
   golden caster sugar
1 lemon
75 g (2½ oz) polenta
2 tsp baking powder
125 g (4½ oz) white spelt flour or
   plain flour
25 g (1 oz) desiccated coconut
3 large eggs
125 ml (4½ fl oz) full-fat milk (or
   non-dairy alternative)

For the topping:
2 tbsp desiccated coconut
2 tbsp coconut oil
3 tbsp coconut cream
2 tbsp agave nectar (or honey)

Preheat the oven to 175°C (350°F). Line an 18-cm (7-in) round cake tin with greaseproof paper.

Soften the coconut oil and coconut cream (in separate bowls) by keeping them in a warm place for 10 minutes. Cream together the coconut oil and sugar, using an electric hand whisk or stand mixer, until pale and fluffy.

Zest the lemon, set aside the zest and extract the juice. Add the juice to the bowl along with the zest, softened coconut cream, sugar mixture, polenta, baking powder, flour and desiccated coconut, and mix well until combined. Whisk together the eggs and milk and slowly add to the cake mixutre, continuously folding, until a soft, wet batter has formed.

Transfer to the cake tin, smooth the surface and bake for 50 minutes or until a skewer inserted into the middle of the cake comes out clean. Leave the cake to cool in the tin.

For the topping, toast the desiccated coconut in a dry frying pan over a medium-high heat until golden. Melt the coconut oil in a double boiler and mix with the coconut cream and agave nectar. Pour over the cake, letting it drizzle down the sides. Sprinkle over the toasted coconut. The cake can be frozen before being iced.

Coconut pie crust

Serves 6–8

60 g (2 oz) coconut oil, plus extra
   for greasing
200 g (7 oz) unsweetened desiccated
   coconut
60 g (2 oz) ground almonds
2 eggs
2 tbsp coconut flour (or increase
   ground almonds to 75 g/2½ oz)
1 tbsp sugar or granulated
   sweetener (optional)

Preheat the oven to 175°C (350°F). Grease a 25-cm (10-in) loose-based springform pie tin generously with coconut oil and line with greaseproof paper.

Melt the coconut oil in a double boiler and add to a food processor with the rest of the ingredients. Blend until the mixture looks crumbly but will stick together when pushed between your fingers.

Transfer the dough to the pie tin and, working from the centre, push the dough around to line the tin in an even layer.

Pre-bake the crust for 20 minutes, or until firm and golden brown. Leave to cool before adding the filling. If using the coconut cream filling (see below), set aside until set. Remove carefully from the pan and serve.

Suggested pie fillings: This pie crust will work well for pumpkin pie, apple pie or custard pie (these will require a further 15–20 minutes cooking once filled). To make a coconut cream filling, whip 250 ml (9 fl oz) double cream with 50 g (2 oz) softened coconut cream. Scoop into the pie crust and spread out. Top with toasted coconut.

Strawberry and vanilla cheesecake

Serves 8

For the base:
75 g (2½ oz) almonds
75 g (2½ oz) dried dates
125 g (4½ oz) rolled oats
100 ml (3½ fl oz) honey
60 g (2 oz) coconut oil

For the filling:
2 x 400 g (14 oz) cans coconut milk
700 g (1 lb 8 oz) strawberries, plus
  extra to decorate
2 tsp vanilla extract
100 ml (3½ fl oz) agave nectar (or
  other liquid sweetener, such as
  honey)
225 g (8 oz) coconut oil

Place the cans of coconut milk in the fridge and leave for at least 2 hours. To make the base, add the almonds to a food processor and blend until finely chopped. Add the dates, oats and honey and blend again. Melt the coconut oil in a double boiler and, with the food processor running, drizzle in the oil until the mixture is starting to combine.

Line a large springform pan with greaseproof paper and press the base mixture down, using your fingers, to achieve a thick layer.

Remove the coconut milk from the fridge and, without shaking the can, remove the top layer of thick coconut cream. Add the coconut cream to a blender or food processor, with the strawberries, vanilla and agave. Blend until smooth.

Melt the coconut oil in a double boiler so it's just melted and not too hot. With the blender or food processor running, drizzle the oil into the coconut cream mixture until fully incorporated.

Pour the filling over the base and smooth the top. Cover with cling film and refrigerate for at least 2 hours until firm. Remove from the pan and serve topped with strawberry slices.

Tips and ideas

The strawberry and vanilla cheesecake filling can be divided between small serving pots and chilled to create individual mousse desserts as an alternative.

Peanut butter cheesecake

Serves 8

For the base:

75 g (2½ oz) almonds
175 g (6 oz) rolled oats
100 ml (3½ fl oz) honey
125 g (4½ oz) crunchy peanut butter
60 g (2 oz) coconut oil

For the filling:
75 g (2½ oz) coconut oil
450 g (1 lb) full-fat cream cheese
   (at room temperature)
125 g (4½ oz) smooth peanut butter
100 ml (3½ fl oz) agave nectar (or
   other liquid sweetener, such as
   maple syrup)
Chocolate magic shell (page 49)
   or melted chocolate, to serve
Chopped peanuts, to decorate

To make the base, place the almonds in a food processor and blend until finely chopped. Add the oats, honey, peanut butter and coconut oil and blend until a crumbly mixture has formed that will stick together when pushed between your fingers.

Line a 18-cm (7-in) springform pan with cling film and press the base mixture down, using your fingers, to achieve a thick layer.

To make the filling, melt the coconut oil and set aside. Combine the rest of the ingredients in a food processor or blender. With the motor running, drizzle in the coconut oil and blend until completely smooth.

Pour the filling on the base and smooth the top. Cover with cling film and refrigerate for at least 2 hours until firm. Remove from the tin and serve drizzled with the chocolate magic shell (page 49) or melted chocolate. Decorate the centre of the cheesecake with chopped peanuts.

Raw cookies and cream cheesecake

Serves 8

For the base:
300 g (10 oz) almonds
350 g (12 oz) dates
1 tbsp coconut oil
2 tbsp cocoa powder

For the filling:
600 g (1 lb 5 oz) cashew nuts
175 ml (6 fl oz) agave nectar (or
   other liquid sweetener, such as
   honey)
175 g (6 oz) coconut oil
100 g (3½ oz) cacao nibs (or
   chopped raw chocolate)

Cover the cashews in water and leave to soak overnight. To make the base, place the almonds in a food processor and process until finely chopped. Add the dates, coconut oil and cocoa powder and blend until the mixture is starting to come together in a ball.

Line a large springform tin with greaseproof paper. Press the base mixture into the bottom of the pan in a thick, even layer. Refrigerate while you prepare the topping.

Drain and rinse the cashews and add them to a food processor or blender with the agave. Melt the coconut oil in a double boiler and drizzle into the cashews, scraping down the sides, as needed. You may need to do this in two batches, depending on the size of your food processor. Add the cacao nibs or raw chocolate and pulse to blend into the mixture.

Pour the filling over the base and smooth the top. Cover with plastic wrap and freeze for at least 6 hours until solid.

To serve, remove from the freezer and springform pan and leave for 20 minutes to soften.

Raspberry and white chocolate mug cake

Serves 1

40 g (1½ oz) plain wholemeal flour
2 tbsp coconut palm sugar or
    granulated sugar
¼ tsp baking powder
2 tbsp coconut oil, plus extra for
    greasing
60 ml (2 fl oz) milk
½ tsp vanilla extract
2 tbsp white chocolate chips
8–10 fresh raspberries

Mix together the flour, sugar and baking powder. Melt the coconut oil in a double boiler. Add the milk and vanilla to the dry ingredients and mix, while drizzling in the coconut oil. Fold in the chocolate chips and raspberries.

Grease a large mug with coconut oil and pour in the batter. Microwave on high for 1½–2 minutes until the cake is firm. Leave to cool before eating.

Chocolate chip mug cake

Serves 1

40 g (1½ oz) plain wholemeal flour
2 tbsp coconut palm sugar
    or granulated sugar
¼ tsp baking powder
2 tbsp coconut oil, plus
    extra for greasing
60 ml (2 fl oz) milk
½ tsp vanilla extract
2 tbsp dark chocolate chips

Mix together the flour, sugar and baking powder in a large bowl. Melt the coconut oil in a double boiler. Add the milk and vanilla to the dry ingredients and mix, while drizzling in the coconut oil. Fold in the chocolate chips.

Grease a large mug with coconut oil and pour in the batter. Microwave on high for 1½–2 minutes, until the cake is firm. Leave to cool before eating.

Cookies

You've got to love the cookie – the easy sweet treat that comes in so many varieties and flavours. Try one of these coconut oil-boosted recipes for a variation of your regular batch.

Chocolate chip cookies

Makes 8–10

150 g (5 oz) plain wholemeal spelt flour
¼ tsp salt
½ tsp baking soda
100 g (3½ oz) caster sugar (or other granulated
   sweetener)
100 g (3½ oz) dark chocolate chips
2 tbsp coconut oil
3–5 tbsp milk (at room temperature)

Preheat the oven to 200°C (400°F). Line a baking tray with greaseproof paper.

Combine the flour, salt, baking soda, sugar and chocolate chips in a large bowl.

Melt the coconut oil in a double boiler and whisk with 3 tbsp. of the milk. Pour into the dry ingredients and mix well. If the mixture seems dry add more milk. The mixture should come together in a soft ball.

Divide the cookie dough into small balls and lightly press down on the baking tray, leaving plenty of room around each, as they will spread out while cooking.

Bake for 7–10 minutes, until the cookies have flattened out. Remove from the oven when they still look slightly underdone, as they will continue to cook on the sheet as they cool.

Leave to cool completely on the baking tray. Store in an airtight container for up to 5 days.

Coconut cookies

Makes 8–10

100 g (3½ oz) white spelt flour or plain white flour
100 g (3½ oz) coconut palm sugar or light brown sugar
75 g (2½ oz) desiccated coconut
125 g (4½ oz) rolled oats
100 g (3½ oz) coconut oil
2 tbsp honey
½ tsp baking soda
2 tbsp boiling water

Preheat the oven to 175°C (350°F). Line a baking tray with greaseproof paper.

Combine the flour, sugar, coconut and oats in a large bowl.

Melt the coconut oil and honey in a double boiler. Mix the baking soda with the water and combine with the melted coconut oil and honey. Make a well in the centre of the dry ingredients and pour in the coconut oil mixture, mixing well to combine.

Divide the dough into balls and lightly press down on the baking tray. Bake in the oven for 15–20 minutes until golden. Leave to cool on the baking tray. Store in an airtight container for up to 1 week.

Peanut butter cookies

Makes 10–12

100 g (3½ oz) smooth peanut butter
150 g (5 oz) coconut palm sugar or
    golden caster sugar
1 egg
½ tsp salt
60 g (2 oz) coconut oil

Preheat the oven to 175°C (350°F). Line a baking tray with greaseproof paper.

Mix the peanut butter, sugar, egg and salt in a large bowl. Melt the coconut oil in a double boiler and pour into the bowl while mixing. Mix until completely combined.

Take heaped tablespoons of the mixture and lightly press down on the baking tray, leaving plenty of room around each, as they will spread out while cooking.

Bake for 10 minutes until the cookies start to brown around the edges. Check regularly as they can burn quickly.

Leave to cool on the baking sheet. Store in an airtight container for up to 1 week.

Oatmeal and raisin cookies

Makes 8

1 medium banana
2 tbsp coconut oil
2 tbsp nut butter (such as peanut
    or almond)
60 g (2 oz) porridge oats
2–3 tbsp raisins

Preheat the oven to 175°C (350°F). Line a baking tray with greaseproof paper.

Mash the banana in a large bowl. Melt the coconut oil in a double boiler, add to the banana and mix well. Add the nut butter and mix well. Mix in the oats and raisins until you have a thick, sticky mixture.

Place heaped tablespoons of the dough on the baking tray and cook for 10 minutes, until beginning to turn golden around the edges.

Leave to cool on the baking tray. Store in an airtight container for up to 5 days.

Tips and ideas

You can experiment with different additions to the cookie recipes. Try adding some chopped nuts or a mix of dried fruit, such as cranberries or goji berries.

Muffins and scones

Whether you love them with your mid-morning coffee or for breakfast, these healthy muffins won't give you a sugar crash. Full of healthy fats from the coconut oil and wholemeal flour, they're the treat you can enjoy guilt free.

Chocolate chip and coconut muffins

Makes 8

150 g (5 oz) wholemeal flour
75 g (2½ oz) coconut palm sugar or light brown sugar
1 tsp baking powder
25 g (1 oz) desiccated coconut
3 eggs (at room temperature)
5 tbsp coconut oil
60 g (2 oz) dark chocolate chips

Preheat the oven to 175°C (350°F). Line a muffin tin with paper liners.

Combine the flour, sugar, baking powder and coconut in a large bowl. Whisk the eggs and mix into the dry ingredients.

Melt the coconut oil in a double boiler and pour into the batter, mixing constantly. Fold in the chocolate chips. Divide the batter between the muffin cases, filling them three-quarters full.

Bake for 20 minutes until the muffins have risen and are golden. A skewer inserted into the centre should come out clean (apart from some melted chocolate). Remove the muffins from the tin and leave to cool on a wire rack.

Store in an airtight container. The muffins will keep for up to 3 days, or can be frozen.

Blueberry muffins

Makes 8

150 g (5 oz) wholemeal flour
75 g (2½ oz) coconut palm sugar or light brown sugar
1 tsp baking powder
3 eggs (at room temperature)
5 tbsp coconut oil
225 g (8 oz) blueberries

Preheat the oven to 175°C (350°F). Line a muffin tin with paper liners.

Combine the flour, sugar and baking powder in a large bowl. Whisk the eggs and mix into the dry ingredients.

Melt the coconut oil in a double boiler and pour into the batter, mixing constantly. Fold in the blueberries. Divide the batter between the muffin cases, filling them three-quarters full.

Bake for 20 minutes until they have risen and are golden brown. A skewer inserted into the centre should come out clean. Remove the muffins from the tin and leave to cool on a wire rack.

Store in an airtight container. The muffins will keep for up to 3 days, or can be frozen.

Courgette muffins

Makes 8

150 g (5 oz) wholemeal flour
75 g (2½ oz) coconut palm sugar or light brown sugar
1 tsp baking powder
3 eggs (at room temperature)
5 tbsp coconut oil
1 courgette

Preheat the oven to 175°C (350°F). Line a muffin tin with paper liners.

Combine the flour, sugar and baking powder in a large bowl. Whisk the eggs and mix into the dry ingredients.

Melt the coconut oil in a double boiler and pour into the batter, while mixing constantly.

Grate the courgette. Place it on a clean tea towel and squeeze to remove the water. Fold the courgette into the muffin batter. Divide the batter between the muffin cases, filling them three-quarters full.

Bake for 25–30 minutes until they have risen and are golden brown. A skewer inserted into the centre should come out clean. Remove the muffins from the tin and leave to cool on a wire rack.

Store in an airtight container. The muffins will keep for up to 3 days, or can be frozen.

Cherry coconut scones

Makes 8

**60 g (2 oz) coconut oil, plus extra
   for greasing**
225 g (8 oz) self-raising flour
60 g (2 oz) caster sugar
60 g (2 oz) desiccated coconut
75 g (2½ oz) glacé cherries
**175 ml (6 fl oz) coconut milk
   beverage (not canned coconut
   milk), plus extra for brushing**

Preheat the oven to 220°C (425°F). Grease a baking tray with coconut oil.

Place the coconut oil and flour in a large bowl and rub together using your fingertips, until the mixture resembles breadcrumbs.

Add the sugar, desiccated coconut and cherries and combine. Add the milk, a little at a time, while kneading the mixture into a soft dough. If it feels sticky, add a little more flour.

Turn the dough out onto a floured surface and roll to 1-cm (½-in) thick. Use a round cookie cutter to cut out several scones, placing them on the baking tray and re-rolling the dough, as needed.

Brush the tops with coconut milk and bake for 10 minutes or until the scones have risen slightly and started to turn golden. Serve warm or leave to cool and store in an airtight container for up to 3 days.

Raisin scones

Makes 8

**60 g (2 oz) coconut oil, plus extra
   for greasing**
225 g (8 oz) self-raising flour
60 g (2 oz) caster sugar
75 g (2½ oz) raisins
**175 ml (6 fl oz) milk, plus extra for
   brushing**

Preheat the oven to 220°C (425°F). Grease a baking tray with coconut oil.

Place the coconut oil and flour in a large bowl and rub together using your fingertips, until the mixture resembles breadcrumbs. Add the sugar and raisins and combine. Add the milk, a little at a time, while kneading the mixture into a soft dough. If it feels sticky, add a little more flour.

Turn the dough out onto a floured surface and roll to 1-cm (½-in) thick. Use a round cookie cutter to cut out several scones, placing them on the prepared baking tray and re-rolling the dough, as needed.

Brush the tops of the scones with a little milk and bake for 10 minutes, or until the scones have risen slightly and started to turn golden. Serve warm or leave to cool and store in an airtight container for up to 3 days.

Variation

Cheese scones: substitute the caster sugar and raisins with 125 g (4½ oz) of grated Cheddar cheese (or a dairy-free alternative).

Sweet treats

Sometimes you just need something sweet and when coconut oil is involved, you won't have an energy crash later on.

Peach and coconut ice cream

Serves 6

3 ripe peaches
1 x 400 g (14 oz) can coconut milk
100 ml (3½ fl oz) honey (or
    alternative liquid sweetener)
60 g (2 oz) coconut oil

This recipe also works well with other soft fruits, such as strawberries, nectarines or plums.

Remove the stones from the peaches and place in a blender with the coconut milk and honey. Blend until smooth.

Melt the coconut oil in a double boiler. With the blender running, pour the oil into the peach mixture in a thin stream, until combined.

Pour the mixture into an ice cream maker and follow the manufacturers' instructions. Alternatively, pour into a suitable freezerproof container and stir by hand every hour until solid.

Remove from the freezer at least 15 minutes before serving to allow the ice cream to soften.

Coconut oil 'butter' icing

Makes enough for a large cake

60 g (2 oz) coconut oil
450 g (1 lb) icing sugar
3–6 tbsp coconut milk

Place the coconut oil in a large mixing bowl and beat with an electric hand whisk or stand mixer until it is softened and becomes fluffy.

Add one-third of the icing sugar and 1 tablespoon of the coconut milk and continue whisking, adding more icing sugar and milk, until the butter icing is thick and creamy.

Coconut bars

Makes 9

225 g (8 oz) coconut oil
200 g (7 oz) desiccated coconut
100 ml (3½ fl oz) honey (or
    alternative liquid sweetener)
¼ tsp salt
200 g (7 oz) dark chocolate
    (optional)

Prepare and line a 20-cm (8 x 8-in) baking tray with greaseproof paper.

Melt the coconut oil in a double boiler. Combine with the desiccated coconut, honey and salt and pour into the prepared tray. Place the tray in the fridge to chill and harden.

Melt the chocolate (if using) in a bowl over a pan of simmering water. Pour over the coconut base and return the tray to the fridge for the chocolate to harden before removing and slicing into squares.

Store in a container in the fridge.

Peanut butter fudge

100 g (3½ oz) coconut oil
125 g (4½ oz) peanut butter
60 ml (2 fl oz) coconut milk
100 ml (3½ fl oz) honey
60 g (2 oz) salted peanuts (optional)

Line a 20-cm (8 x 8-in) baking tray with cling film.

Melt the coconut oil in a double boiler and combine with the peanut butter, coconut milk and honey. Stir in the peanuts (if using). Pour into the prepared tray and transfer to the fridge to harden.

Once solid, remove from the sheet and cut into 9 squares.

The fudge will keep in the fridge for 1 month or in the freezer for 6 months.

Almond and raisin fudge

40 g (1½ oz) raisins
75 ml (2½ fl oz) rum (optional)
100 g (3½ oz) coconut oil
125 g (4½ oz) almond butter
60 ml (2 fl oz) coconut milk
100 ml (3½ fl oz) honey
40 g (1½ oz) almonds

Soak the raisins in the rum overnight and drain the following morning. If not using rum, soak in hot water for 5 minutes to plump.

Line a small loaf tin with cling film.

Melt the coconut oil in a double boiler and combine with the almond butter, coconut milk and honey. Roughly chop the almonds and stir in with the raisins. Pour into the prepared tin and transfer to the fridge to harden.

Once solid, remove from the pan and cut into 9 squares.

The fudge will keep in the fridge for 1 month or in the freezer for 6 months.

Vanilla almond fudge

100 g (3½ oz) coconut oil
125 ml (4½ fl oz) almond butter
60 ml (2 fl oz) coconut milk
100 ml (3½ fl oz) honey
2 tsp vanilla extract
1 tsp vanilla paste (optional)

Line a 20-cm (8 x 8-in) baking tray with cling film.

Melt the coconut oil in a double boiler and combine with the almond butter, coconut milk, honey, vanilla extract and vanilla paste (if using). Pour into the prepared tray and transfer to the fridge to harden.

Once solid, remove from the sheet and cut into 9 squares.

The fudge will keep in the fridge for 1 month or in the freezer for 6 months.

Chocolate chip cookie dough fudge

100 g (3½ oz) coconut oil
125 g (4½ oz) cashew butter
60 ml (2 fl oz) coconut milk
100 ml (3½ fl oz) honey
1 tsp vanilla extract
75 g (2½ oz) dark chocolate chips

Line a 20-cm (8 x 8-in) baking tray with cling film.

Melt the coconut oil in a double boiler and combine with the cashew butter, coconut milk, honey and vanilla. Lightly stir in the chocolate chips (make sure the mixture isn't too hot or the chocolate chips will melt and spread through the fudge). Pour into the prepared tray and transfer to the fridge to harden.

Once solid, remove from the tray and cut into 9 squares.

The fudge will keep in the fridge for 1 month or in the freezer for 6 months.

Confectionery

Rather than satisfying your sweet tooth with sugar, try these naturally sweetened coconut oil-based sweets. They'll not only quash sugar cravings but will also help fill you up, so great for kids as well.

Coconut mints

Makes 12–15

100 g (3½ oz) coconut oil
60 g (2 oz) coconut butter
    (or manna)
100 ml (3¼ fl oz) honey
½ tsp peppermint extract
    (or culinary grade peppermint
    essential oil)

Melt the coconut oil in a double boiler and stir in the coconut butter and honey. Add the peppermint extract (or 1–2 drops at a time of peppermint essential oil, to taste).

Pour into a suitable silicone mould and refrigerate until solid. Pop out of the mould and store in an airtight container in the fridge for up to 1 month.

Salted caramels

Makes 12–15

175 g (6 oz) dried dates
60 ml (2 fl oz) coconut milk
100 ml (3½ fl oz) honey
1 tsp salt
100 g (3½ oz) coconut oil

Soak the dates in water for 2 hours then drain. Place in a blender or food processor with the coconut milk, maple syrup and salt. Blend until smooth.

Melt the coconut oil in a double boiler. With the blender or processor running, drizzle the oil into the date mixture until combined.

Pour into a suitable silicone mould and refrigerate until solid. Pop out of the mould and store in an airtight container in the fridge for up to 1 month.

Raspberry ripple sweets

Makes 12–15

100 g (3 ½ oz) coconut oil
125 g (4 ½ oz) raspberries
100 ml (3 ½ fl oz) honey (or
    alternative liquid sweetener)

Melt the coconut oil in a double boiler and pour into a blender with the raspberries and honey. Blend until smooth. Strain the mixture through a fine sieve to remove the raspberry seeds.

Pour into a suitable silicone mould and refrigerate until solid. Pop out of the mould and store in an airtight container in the fridge for up to 1 month.

Health

WHEN YOU CONSIDER coconut oil's many reputed benefits, it's easy to see why it's such an incredible product for addressing a multitude of health needs. It is natural, free of chemicals, antibacterial and antifungal, which makes it particularly suitable for using on delicate baby skin and for treating the skin of mums and mums-to-be.

Coconut oil's healing properties are also perfect for treating common skin complaints such as eczema and sunburn, along with soothing a number of other ailments. Its versatility also makes it the ideal base for creams and balms that can be used for everything from treating grazes to making throat lozenges.

But coconut oil is not only beneficial for the skin; it also has a number of benefits for the digestive system – from supporting gut health and eradicating parasites to relieving heartburn. And, when it comes to preventing and supporting the recovery of illnesses like colds and flu, coconut oil's antiviral properties are well placed to support the body's immune system.

With its amazing array of benefits it's time for coconut oil to take its place in your first aid kit.

General health

From moisturiser and skin cleanser to health-boosting teas and oil-pulling capsules, the following preparations highlight the incredible diversity of coconut oil.

Supplement booster

Many of the vitamins and minerals in our supplements are best absorbed by the body alongside fat, which makes coconut oil a brilliant supplement booster. Just take 1 tablespoon of coconut oil alongside your regular supplements to boost their uptake in the body.

Blood sugar balancer

Coconut oil's high fat content makes it perfect for helping to balance blood sugar levels, as it will supply energy to the body while having no adverse impact on blood sugar. Simply take 1–2 tablespoons of coconut oil when you need an energy boost, or to balance blood sugar.

Good sleep treatment

Due to coconut oil's balancing impact on the body's energy levels, it makes a superb sleep treatment. Take 1–2 tablespoons of coconut oil just before you go to bed to help you enjoy a good night's sleep.

Ear-cleaning oil

Coconut oil is a great product to use for cleaning your ears. Add a small amount to the end of a cotton bud and gently wipe around the outer ear to clean it. Don't push the cotton bud into your ear canal.

Magnesium body butter

A lack of magnesium can contribute to muscle weakness and cramps, tiredness and memory loss. Magnesium is well absorbed through the skin and this magnesium body butter is a great way to relieve sore muscles by getting magnesium to exactly where it's needed, while also moisturising the skin.

60 g (2 oz) coconut oil
25 g (1 oz) shea butter
60 ml (2 fl oz) magnesium oil
  (see tip below)
5–10 drops lavender essential oil (optional)

Melt the coconut oil and shea butter in a double boiler. Leave to cool until the oils are no longer liquid and are starting to turn opaque.

Using a stand mixer or electric mixer, whip the oils, while slowly pouring in the magnesium oil and adding the lavender essential oils (if using).

Place the mixture in the fridge to chill for about 20 minutes before whipping again. The cream should have a thick, fluffy texture.

Transfer to a jar or airtight container and store in a cool place.

Healing Epsom salt bath treatment

Epsom salt – or magnesium sulphate – is a naturally occurring mineral high in magnesium. When added to a bath, the salts are broken down and the magnesium is absorbed into the body. This helps to relax muscles and relieve pain. To increase the benefits, try this healing bath treatment with added coconut oil.

300 g (10 oz) Epsom salts (increase if your bath tub is
  large)
100 g (3½ oz) coconut oil
6–12 drops lavender essential oil

Fill the bath with hot water (as hot as is comfortable for you). Add the Epsom salt, coconut oil and lavender essential oil.

Metabolism–boosting tea

Coconut oil's metabolism-boosting properties are enhanced when added to green tea, which is another metabolism-boosting superfood. Green tea is packed with antioxidants that support good health and studies have shown that green tea can increase the metabolic rate. This recipe is a simple and delicious way to give your metabolism a boost.

Serves 1
1 green tea bag or 1 tsp loose-leaf green tea
1 tbsp coconut oil

Brew the green tea with hot water and add the coconut oil by whisking it into the tea.

Tips and ideas

You can purchase ready-mixed magnesium oil which isn't actually an oil, more a thick liquid or you can make your own by combining half a cup of filtered water and half a cup of magnesium chloride flakes.

Inflammation-fighting capsules

1.5-cm (½-in) piece ginger root
100 g (3½ oz) coconut oil
2 tsp turmeric
2 tbsp honey

Many ailments create, or are caused by, inflammation in the body. These capsules are a handy way to take natural foods with anti-inflammatory compounds every day.

Peel and finely grate the ginger. Melt the coconut oil in a double boiler and mix with the grated ginger, turmeric and honey.

Mix well and pour into small silicone moulds (that hold around ½ tablespoon) and leave to cool.

Pop the capsules out of the moulds and store in a jar in a cool place. Can be eaten or sucked daily to enjoy anti-inflammatory benefits.

Oil pulling

Oil pulling is the ancient Ayurvedic technique of swilling the mouth with oil. It is reputed to help draw out toxins, clean and whiten the teeth and protect the gums from disease. Coconut oil is ideal for oil pulling, as it has the added benefit of being naturally antibacterial.

Oil pulling can be as simple as taking a spoonful of coconut oil off the spoon and swilling it around your mouth for as long as possible (practiced oil pullers swill the oil around for up to 20 minutes!) before spitting it into the bin (never the basin or you risk clogging your drains).

To make oil pulling more convenient and tasty, try creating your own oil-pulling capsules.

Flavoured oil-pulling capsules

225 g (8 oz) coconut oil
Essential oils (see flavours)

Melt the coconut oil in a double boiler. Add the essential oils to the coconut oil and stir.

Pour the liquid coconut oil into a mould and refrigerate until solid. Pop the oil-pulling capsules out of the mould and store in a glass jar in the fridge for easy oil pulling.

Flavors

Peppermint: add 5–10 drops of peppermint essential oil.

Cinnamon and clove: add 5 drops of cinnamon essential oil and 2 drops of clove essential oil.

Lemon: add 5–10 drops of lemon essential oil.

Parent and baby

Coconut oil is the perfect product to use with babies due to its natural antibacterial and antifungal properties. It's very gentle on delicate baby skin and is especially suited to several common baby skin complaints.

Cradle cap

To relieve cradle cap, lightly cover the affected area with a coating of coconut oil. Leave to absorb for at least 1 hour then use a soft brush to remove the scales. Repeat as needed.

Chicken pox relief

To relieve the itch of chicken pox sores, apply a light coating of coconut oil as and when required.

Nipple cream

To soothe cracked nipples, apply coconut oil as and when required to promote healing and offer relief.

Baby lotion

Coconut oil can be used straight from the jar as a nourishing and safe skin oil for babies. However, it's also useful to have a lighter lotion as well.

75 g (2½ oz) coconut oil
125 g (4½ oz) aloe vera gel
5–10 drops baby safe essential oil, such as lavender (optional)

Melt the coconut oil in a double boiler and leave to cool and solidify slightly for 10 minutes.

Blend using a stick blender and add the aloe vera gel and essential oil (if using).

Transfer the lotion to a jar or airtight container and store in a cool place.

Stretch mark treatment

Unfortunately, stretch marks are a routine part of pregnancy. Here are some nourishing creams and oils for soothing stretched skin and supporting elasticity to reduce scarring.

Coconut oil can be used straight from the jar for an effective stretch-mark prevention and treatment. Simply massage into the area as needed.

Cocoa butter stretch mark cream

100 g (3½ oz) coconut oil
60 g (2 oz) cocoa butter

Melt the coconut oil and cocoa butter in a double boiler. Leave the mixture to cool until it is no longer liquid.

Whip the mixture, using a stand mixer or electric hand mixer, until thick and fluffy. Transfer to a jar and store at room temperature.

Frankincense and lavender stretch mark oil

100 g (3½ oz) fractionated coconut oil
2 tbsp vitamin E oil
10 drops frankincense essential oil
10 drops lavender essential oil

Combine all the ingredients in a bottle. Apply liberally, as required.

Nappy cream

60 g (2 oz) coconut oil
25 g (1 oz) shea butter
1 tbsp. arrowroot powder

Melt the coconut oil and shea butter in a double boiler. Leave in a cool place until the oils are no longer liquid and are just beginning to turn opaque.

Add the arrowroot and whip, using a stand mixer or electric hand mixer. Transfer to a jar or airtight container and store in a cool place.

Variation

Lavender: add 5 drops of lavender essential oil to promote healing.

Calendula nappy balm

60 g (2 oz) coconut oil
25 g (1 oz) shea butter
60 g (2 oz) calendula-infused oil
Pinch of turmeric powder (optional)

Melt the coconut oil and beeswax in a double boiler. Combine with the calendula oil and turmeric (if using).

Pour into tins or a small glass jar. Store in a cool place.

Tips and ideas

If you're pregnant or think you might be pregnant, always check whether an essential oil is suitable for use.

Skin complaints

Coconut oil's skin-softening and protective qualities make it an excellent product to use for a range of skin complaints. It can help to relieve the symptoms of eczema, rashes and sunburn, among other ailments.

Tattoo salve

Coconut oil makes an excellent post-tattoo treatment. Apply a very thin layer of coconut oil to your tattoo after it has been washed in fresh, clean water. Repeat three to four times a day until it has healed.

Skin rash treatment

Treat skin rashes with a light layer of coconut oil to soothe itching and irritation and promote healing.

Hangnail softener

If you have one of those annoying tough pieces of skin at the side of your nail, try softening it with a dab of coconut oil. The oil will help to prevent it catching or becoming sore.

Ingrown hair treatment

To soften the skin around ingrown hairs, apply a coating of coconut oil. Leave the oil on for a couple of hours before extracting the hair with tweezers.

Honey graze salve

Like coconut oil, honey is naturally antibacterial and antiseptic so it's a perfect ingredient in this graze salve.

60 g (2 oz) coconut oil
2 tbsp beeswax
1 tbsp honey

Melt the coconut oil and beeswax in a double boiler. Add the honey and stir to combine.

Pour into a small jar and leave to cool and solidify. Store in a cool place.

Eczema cream

Eczema is a condition that causes dry, red, scaly and itchy skin. This cream uses honey and essential oils, alongside coconut oil, to soothe and moisturise areas of eczema.

100 g (3½ oz) coconut oil
60 g (2 oz) shea butter
2 tbsp honey
5–10 drops lavender essential oil
5–10 drops tea tree essential oil

Melt the coconut oil and shea butter in a double boiler. Add the honey and stir to combine then add the essential oils and mix well.

Leave the mixture to cool until it's no longer liquid and is starting to turn opaque. Blend with a stick blender until a creamy texture is reached.

Transfer to a jar and store in a cool place.

Cooling aloe vera and coconut gel cream

75 g (2½ oz) coconut oil
125 g (4½ oz) aloe vera gel
1 tbsp witch hazel
20 drops peppermint essential oil

Melt the coconut oil in a double boiler. Leave to cool for 10 minutes. Add the aloe vera gel and blend together with a stick blender.

While blending, stop to add the witch hazel and peppermint essential oil. Blend until a creamy texture has been reached.

Transfer to a jar or airtight container and store in a cool place. The cream can be kept in the fridge and applied cool to skin but the texture will be a little firmer.

Honey and lavender sunburn salve

60 g (2 oz) coconut oil
1 tbsp beeswax
100 g (3½ oz) thick set honey
20 drops lavender essential oil

Melt the coconut oil, beeswax and honey in a double boiler. Add the lavender essential oil and stir to combine.

Transfer the mixture to a small jar and leave to cool and harden. Store in a cool place.

Keratosis pilaris scrub bars

100 g (3½ oz) coconut oil
2 tbsp beeswax
1 tbsp honey
60 g (2 oz) soft brown sugar
10 drops lemon essential oil

Melt the coconut oil and beeswax in a double boiler. Add the honey, sugar and lemon essentail oil and mix well. Pour the mixture into a silicone mould and leave to harden.

In the shower or bath, rub the bar into areas of keratosis pilaris and massage gently. Rinse off and moisturise with a coconut oil body butter (page 73).

Colds and flu

Coconut oil is an excellent addition to your cold and flu-fighting collection. With its natural antiviral qualities, it is superbly placed to help your body fight illness and boost your immune system.

Cough relief

Take 1–3 teaspoons of coconut oil straight from the jar to ease a dry cough.

Cough syrup

2 tbsp coconut oil
4 tbsp runny honey
2 tbsp elderberry syrup (optional)
1 lemon

Melt the coconut oil in a double boiler and stir in the honey and elderberry syrup (if using). Juice the lemon and mix in the juice.

Store the syrup at room temperature in a jar, taking 1–2 teaspoons up to 5 times a day for cough and sore throat relief.

Vapour rub

60 g (2 oz) coconut oil
2 tbsp cocoa butter
1 tbsp beeswax
20–30 drops eucalyptus essential oil
5–10 drops peppermint essential oil
5–10 drops lavender essential oil
5 drops tea tree oil essential oil

Melt the coconut oil, cocoa butter and beeswax in a double boiler. Add the essential oils and stir to combine.

Pour the mixture into a small jar and leave to solidify. Store in a cool place.

Decongestant bombs

1 tbsp coconut oil
225 g (8 oz) baking soda
75 ml (2½ fl oz) water
10–20 drops eucalyptus essential oil
5–10 drops peppermint essential oil
5–10 drops tea tree essential oil

Melt the coconut oil in a double boiler. In a separate bowl mix together the baking soda and water until a paste forms.

Add the melted coconut oil, stirring constantly, followed by the essential oils.

Divide the mixture into silicone moulds and leave for at least 24 hours to dry out. Pop the bombs out of the moulds and store in an airtight container.

Tips and ideas

Pop one of these in your shower to enjoy the benefits of breathe-easy essential oils. Just ensure you don't slip if the floor of the shower becomes oily!

Lemon, ginger and honey drink

Serves 4

2 lemons
5-cm (2-in) piece fresh ginger
4 tbsp honey
4 tbsp coconut oil
700 ml (24 fl oz) water

Squeeze the juice from the lemons into a pan. Peel the ginger root and cut into thin slices. Add to the pan with the honey and coconut oil.

Add the water and bring to a simmer. Leave the pan over a low heat so the ginger infuses.

To drink, fill a cup two-thirds full and top up with hot water from a kettle. Drink throughout the day.

Elderberry tea

Serves 1

1 elderberry tea bag
1 tbsp coconut oil
1 tbsp honey

Brew the elderberry tea. Add the coconut oil and honey and stir to combine.

Honey and lemon throat drops

Makes 10–15

100 g (3½ oz) coconut oil
175 g (6 oz) set honey
Juice of 1 lemon

Soften the coconut oil (but do not melt completely) by leaving it in a warm place for 10–20 minutes.

Transfer to a stand mixer or separate bowl and whip, using an electric hand mixer. Add the honey, followed by the lemon juice and continue to mix.

Transfer the mixture into small silicone moulds or place 1 teaspoon balls of the mix on a baking tray lined with greaseproof paper.

Freeze the drops until they become solid, remove from the moulds and store in a jar in the fridge.

Variations

Cinnamon throat drops: substitute the lemon juice with 1 teaspoon of ground cinnamon.

Elderberry throat drops: substitute the lemon juice with 60 ml (2 fl. oz.) of elderberry syrup.

Ginger and clove throat drops

Makes 10–15

2.5-cm (1-in) piece fresh ginger
100 g (3½ oz) coconut oil
175 g (6 oz) set honey
¼ tsp ground cloves

Peel and grate or finely chop the ginger. Set aside.

Soften the coconut oil (but do not melt completely) by leaving it in a warm place for 10–20 minutes. Transfer to a stand mixer or separate bowl and whip, using an electric hand mixer. Add the honey and continue to mix, then add the minced ginger and ground cloves.

Transfer the mixture into small silicone moulds or place 1 teaspoon balls of the mix on a baking tray lined with greaseproof paper. Freeze the drops until they become solid, remove from moulds and store in a jar in the refrigerator.

Digestion

Indigestion, heartburn and other digestive ailments can cause discomfort. These natural preparations will help to relieve the symptoms without resorting to the medicine cabinet. They all make use of the health properties of coconut oil and are combined with other natural ingredients.

Food-poisoning relief

When you're experiencing food poisoning you probably won't want to eat anything. However, getting 1–2 tablespoons of coconut oil into your stomach will help your body heal. Coconut oil passes very quickly through the stomach, so it will keep your energy levels up when you can't face other food and will also support the transit of any bacteria out of your system.

Heartburn treatment

Coconut oil's anti-inflammatory properties work to soothe the digestive tract and settle your stomach, reducing the extra stomach acid. Try taking 1–2 tablespoons of coconut oil when heartburn strikes.

Handy constipation relief capsules

Coconut oil is excellent for digestion and when combined with the fibrous prune, it makes a sweet digestive aid to get things moving.

175 g (6 oz) dried prunes
75 g (2½ oz) coconut oil

Place the dried prunes in a food processor and process for 2 minutes. Add the coconut oil and continue to process until the mixture comes together in one doughy ball.

Remove from the food processor and roll the mixture into several small balls or press into small silicone moulds. Store in the refrigerator. Take 1–2 capsules, as required.

Gas-relieving tea

Coconut oil can help relieve gas and a bloated stomach. When combined with specific herbal teas it can help relax your body.

1 peppermint or camomile tea bag
1 tbsp coconut oil

Brew the tea in hot water. Whisk in the coconut oil and drink.

Anti-sickness chews

Ginger has potent anti-nausea properties. Use these anti-sickness chews whenever you feel nauseous to get some relief.

1.5-cm (½-in) piece fresh ginger
100 g (3½ oz) coconut oil
175 g (6 oz) set honey

Peel and grate, mince or finely chop the ginger, then set aside.

Soften the coconut oil (but not melt completely) by leaving it in a warm place for 10–20 minutes.

Transfer to a stand mixer or separate bowl and whip, using an electric hand mixer. Add the honey and continue to mix, then add the ginger.

Transfer the mixture into small silicone moulds or place 1 teaspoon balls of the mix on a baking tray lined with greaseproof paper. Freeze the drops until they become solid, remove from the moulds and store in a jar in the refrigerator.

Ailments

Coconut oil should take a prominent place in your medicine drawer as it can be used to alleviate all manner of ailments. When combined with arnica gel it can make an effective bruise cream; it can help to treat cold sores; relieve headaches; and ease the discomfort of dandruff.

Anti-yeast treatment

Coconut oil's antifungal properties make it the perfect natural treatment for yeast infections of any kind. Apply coconut oil regularly to the infected area.

Dandruff treatment

Dandruff can cause an itchy and uncomfortable scalp, as well as pesky white flakes of skin. To ease discomfort and treat the skin, massage a small amount of coconut oil into the scalp. Leave it for a few minutes – or overnight – then shampoo to remove any residue. Repeat as needed.

Dry nose/nostril treatment

During the winter months when the air becomes drier, or if you're fighting a cold, the nose can become sore and dry. Try applying a thin layer of coconut oil to the outside and inside of your nose to hydrate and soften the area.

Cold sore treatment

Coconut oil is a useful treatment for cold sores. Apply directly to the affected area as soon as you feel the blister starting to form and repeat as needed.

Ear infection treatment

To treat ear infections place 2–3 drops of liquid coconut oil into the ear canal. Tip your head to the side and leave it there for a couple of minutes to allow the coconut oil to penetrate, then repeat on the other side.

Haemorrhoids

Apply coconut oil to areas affected by haemorrhoids to soothe the area, especially before using the bathroom.

Athlete's foot treatment

Apply coconut oil directly to the affected area daily until the fungus dies off.

Bruise cream with arnica gel

Arnica is a herb that can help with muscle soreness and bruising of the skin. Applied with coconut oil, it will help to take the sting out of bruises, reduce inflammation and help the area to heal more quickly.

100 g (3½ oz) coconut oil
125 g (4½ oz) arnica gel

Melt the coconut oil in a double boiler then leave to cool for 5-10 minutes until the oil is just beginning to become opaque again.

Add the arnica gel and mix, using a stand mixer or electric hand mixer, until completely combined.

Transfer the cream to a jar and store in a cool place.

Headache salve

60 g (2 oz) coconut oil
25 g (1 oz) beeswax
5–10 drops lavender essential oil
5–10 drops Roman camomile
    essential oil

Melt the coconut oil and
beeswax in a double boiler. Add
the essential oils and transfer the
mixture to a small jar or tin.

Leave to harden and store in
a cool place.

Tips and ideas

Coconut oil makes an
excellent carrier for
essential oils that ease
headaches. Try rubbing
a little of this salve into
your temples to relieve
pain and aid relaxation.

Sports

Whether you use coconut oil to make delicious energy shots and sports drinks or use it to relieve sore muscles after a workout, your sports regime will be enhanced by the wide-reaching benefits of this incredible ingredient.

Chafe protector

Coconut oil can help prevent against chafing skin on long runs. Apply a thin layer of coconut oil, as needed, to lubricate the area.

Sore muscle rubs

This sore muscle rub contains arnica gel and selected essential oils for relieving aches and pains. Choose between warming and cooling blends, according to preference. The cooling blend is best for areas you think may be inflamed, such as joints like the knees and elbows. The warming blend is excellent for areas of general soreness after a run, such as the thighs.

Warming sore muscle rub

100 g (3½ oz) coconut oil
40 g (1½ oz) beeswax
75 g (2½ oz) arnica gel
10–20 drops cinnamon
    essential oil
10–20 drops ginger essential oil

Melt the coconut oil and beeswax in a double boiler then leave to cool until the oils are no longer liquid and have just started to turn opaque (around 10–20 minutes).

Add the arnica gel and essential oils and mix well to combine.

Transfer the mixture to a jar and leave to set. Store in a cool place.

Cooling sore muscle rub

100 g (3½ oz) coconut oil
40 g (1½ oz) beeswax
75 g (2½ oz) arnica gel
10–20 drops peppermint essential oil
10–20 drops eucalyptus essential oil

Melt the coconut oil and beeswax in a double boiler. Leave to cool until the oils are no longer liquid and have just started to turn opaque (around 10–20 minutes).

Add the arnica gel and essential oils and mix well to combine. Transfer the mixture to a jar and leave to set. Store in a cool place.

Natural energy shots

Dates are an excellent natural source of carbohydrates. Try these sweet-tasting energy shots, which are perfect before or during a workout – I used these when I was training for a half-marathon. Simply wrap in foil and keep in your pocket to eat for a mid-run boost.

Date and coconut energy shots

175 g (6 oz) dried dates
75 g (2½ oz) coconut oil
2 tbsp desiccated coconut

Add all the ingredients to a food processor and process until the mixture forms a smooth ball with a doughy texture. Roll the mixture into balls and store in the fridge.

Lemon and orange energy shots

175 g (6 oz) dried dates
75 g (2½ oz) coconut oil
Zest of 1 lemon
Zest of 1 orange

Add all the ingredients to a food processor and
process until the mixture forms a smooth ball with
a doughy texture. Roll the mixture into balls and
store in the fridge.

Lemon and lime sports drink

Serves 2

1 lemon
1 lime
475 ml (16 fl oz) coconut water
1 tbsp chia seeds
1 tbsp coconut oil

Juice the lemon and lime and add to the coconut
water. Pour into a blender along with the chia
seeds and coconut oil.

Blend well until the mixture is frothy. Serve
immediately or pour into a bottle to take with you.

The drink can be kept in the fridge but it may
need re-blending before drinking.

Orange sports drink

Serves 2

240 ml (8½ fl oz) orange juice
240 ml (8½ fl oz) coconut water
1 tbsp chia seeds
1 tbsp coconut oil

Add the orange juice and coconut water to a
blender, followed by the chia seeds and coconut oil.

Blend well until the mixture is frothy. Serve
immediately or pour into a bottle to take with you.

The drink can be kept in the fridge but it may need
re-blending before drinking.

Strawberry sports drink

Serves 2

225 g (8 oz) fresh strawberries
350 ml (12 fl oz) coconut water
1 tbsp chia seeds
1 tbsp coconut oil

Add the strawberries and coconut water to a
blender followed by the chia seeds and coconut oil.

Blend well until the mixture is frothy. Serve
immediately or pour into a bottle to take with you.

The drink can be kept in the fridge but it may need
re-blending before drinking.

Insect bite treatment and repellent

Coconut oil can both soothe the skin around insect bites and act as an effective insect repellent.

Bite and sting treatment balm

60 g (2 oz) coconut oil
2 tbsp beeswax
1 tbsp honey
5–10 drops lavender essential oil
5 drops peppermint essential oil
5 drops tea tree essential oil

Melt the coconut oil and beeswax in a double boiler.

Add the honey and stir until it dissolves into the coconut oil. Add the essential oils and transfer to a small jar or tin.

Leave to solidify and store in a cool place.

Bite and sting treatment roll-on

2 tbsp fractionated coconut oil
10 drops lavender essential oil
5 drops peppermint essential oil
5 drops tea tree essential oil

Combine all of the oils and transfer to a small roll-on bottle.

Insect repellent bars

100 g (3½ oz) coconut oil
40 g (1½ oz) beeswax
2 tbsp cocoa butter
Essential oils (see below)

Melt the coconut oil, beeswax and cocoa butter in a double boiler. Add the essential oils and pour into silicone moulds.

Leave to cool and harden in the fridge. Pop out of the moulds and store in a cool place.

To use, gently rub the bar over exposed skin to keep insects at bay.

Citronella oil: citronella is a commonly used insect repellent. Use between 10–20 drops of citronella essential oil and 5–10 drops of lavender essential oil.

Peppermint: peppermint is a natural mosquito deterrent. Use 10–20 drops of peppermint essential oil.

Aromatherapy and stress relief

Don't let a stressful day get you dow – use coconut oil to create relaxing balms and burner melts and you'll wind down in no time at all.

Aromatherapy burner melts

These melts are designed to be used with essential oil burners so you can create ready-to-use blends with no water needed. Just place a melt in the top of the burner and enjoy the amazing scent.

100 g (3½ oz) coconut oil per blend
Essential oils (see blends below)

Melt the coconut oil in a double boiler. Add the essential oils and stir well to combine.

Pour the liquid coconut oil into small moulds (ensure the size of the mould is suitable for the size of the burner you intend to use) and leave to harden in the refrigerator.

Pop the burners out of the moulds and store in a jar in a cool place.

Blends
Sleep blend: cedarwood, lavender and orange essential oils.

De-stress blend: geranium, lavender and rose essential oils.

Uplifting blend: orange, lemon and peppermint essential oils.

Anti-sickness blend: lime, peppermint, tea tree and eucalyptus essential oils.

Experiment with how much oil you use; try 5–10 drops as a starting point.

Lavender and geranium stress-relieving balm

100 g (3½ oz) coconut oil
10 drops lavender essential oil
10 drops geranium essential oil

Melt the coconut oil in a double boiler and add the essential oils. Transfer to a small jar or tin and leave to cool and solidify.

To use, rub your fingers into the balm then massage onto the skin.

Store at room temperature to keep the balm quite hard, or warm it before using for a softer texture.

Mandarin and ylang ylang stress-relieving oil

100 g (3½ oz) fractionated coconut oil
10 drops mandarin essential oil
10 drops ylang ylang essential oil

Combine the oils and transfer to a bottle. Store in a cool place.

Note: mandarin essential oil can be replaced with wild orange essential oil, if liked.

Tips and ideas
Many essential oils have stress-relieving benefits and coconut oil is the perfect carrier oil to deliver them. Try one of these oil rubs in a self-massage to enjoy the benefits.

Household

SOME OF THE MOST surprising coconut oil uses are those around the home. As a natural oil with lubricating and protective barrier properties, it can be put to use in many ways, with applications in every room of the house – not to mention the garden and even the car!

As coconut oil is completely natural, it forms a safe base for a range of products and preparations for kids and pets and is well suited for use in cleaning preparations that are free from chemicals such as sprays, laundry soap and detergent.

All of the following uses and preparations can be made with virgin or extra virgin coconut oil. However, if you're looking to save money, refined coconut oil can be used where the oil is being employed as a lubricant for machinery.

Around the home

There are so many ways that coconut oil can help with daily household chores – and it saves clogging up the cupboards with lots of different polishes, cleaners and treatments.

Leather treatment

Use a soft cloth to rub neat coconut oil onto leather furniture or clothing to keep it supple, clean and moisturised. Always do a patch test first, especially on dyed or coloured leather.

Wood treatment

Coconut oil can be applied to wood to give it a protective coating. Use a cloth to apply the coconut oil in a circular motion.

Hinge lubricant

Squeaking hinges? Apply neat coconut oil to a hinge to lubricate it and assist with easy movement of the parts.

Chewing gum remover

Apply liberal amounts of coconut oil to the chewing gum, leave for 5 minutes then gently remove using a cloth. Clean the area with castile soap to remove any remaining oil.

Label remover

Do you hate it when the glue from a label won't come off? Apply coconut oil and leave for 5 minutes then it will be easier to rub or scrape off.

Rust remover

Spread a little coconut oil over the rusty area. Leave for 2–3 hours and then wipe off with a cloth. Rub in a little extra coconut oil around the rest of the metal to protect it from becoming rusty in the future.

Unstick zips

If you have a zip that sticks easily or doesn't run smoothly, spread a thin layer of coconut oil along the teeth of each side of the zip, then run the zip up and down a few times to lubricate it.

Remove tight jewellery

Rings getting stuck on your fingers? Use coconut oil as a lubricant to ease them off.

Condition guitar strings

Coconut oil can be used to keep guitar strings conditioned and supple. Place a small amount of coconut oil on a soft cloth and run down each string.

Furniture polish

Use coconut oil as a general furniture polish, applied with a soft cloth. Always patch test on an inconspicuous corner first.

Shoe polish

To clean, polish and condition leather shoes, apply coconut oil with a soft cloth and buff the shoes to a shine.

Shine jewellery

Use coconut oil to clean and shine jewelery. Just add a little coconut oil to a soft cloth and polish the jewelery to a shine.

Houseplant polish

Houseplant leaves become dusty over time. Lightly rub large leaves with a little coconut oil on a soft cloth to remove dust and keep them shiny.

Wardrobe hanging rail

Remove all your clothes from the wardrobe and glide a little coconut oil along the rail to help the hangers slide easily along it.

Lubricate scissors

Keep your scissors working effectively with a dab of coconut oil on the moving parts.

Stop wax sticking to candle holders

To make it easy to remove melted wax from candleholders, gently rub a layer of coconut oil all over them to form a barrier and prevent the wax from sticking.

Prevent rust forming inside jar lids

To prevent jar lids becoming rusty, apply a layer of coconut oil to create a protective barrier.

Unclog spray bottle nozzles

Apply coconut oil to the nozzle and leave for 5 minutes then rub off with a cloth.

Cleaning

Coconut oil makes an excellent addition to your cleaning cupboard. Try one of these simple preparations for effective, natural and toxin-free cleaning.

Multipurpose spray cleaner

475 ml (16 fl oz) boiled and cooled water
1 tbsp castile soap
1 tbsp fractionated coconut oil
Essential oils (see blends)

Combine the boiled water, castile soap, coconut oil and your chosen essential oil in a spray bottle. Shake before use.

Blends

Citrus: 5–10 drops lemon essential oil and 5–10 drops tea tree essential oil.

Lavender: 5–10 drops lavender essential oil and 5–10 drops tea tree essential oil.

Make-up and hairbrush cleaner

60 g (2 oz) coconut oil
10 drops tea tree essential oil
Castile soap

Soften the coconut oil in a warm place and mix in the tea tree essential oil.

Gently massage into the bristles of brushes to loosen make-up, dirt and other oils. Rinse in hot water with 1–2 drops of castile soap to remove any remaining oil. Leave to dry on a flat surface.

Soap scum cleaner

Use coconut oil straight from the jar with a scrubbing brush for easy removal of soap scum around the bath and sink.

Stain remover

1 tbsp coconut oil
1 tbsp baking soda

Combine the coconut oil and baking soda (softening the coconut oil first, if needed) and scrub into the stained area with a small brush, such as an old toothbrush.

Wash the clothing as usual or use some castile soap first to remove any excess oil.

Brush cleaner

Coconut oil is especially helpful for cleaning brushes that have been used with oil-based products, as the clean coconut oil can break down the 'dirty' oils on the brushes.

Paintbrush cleaner

Use coconut oil straight from the jar to remove oil-based paint and emulsion paint from paintbrushes. Once the coconut oil has loosened the paint, rinse in hot water with a drop of castile soap and follow with a white vinegar rinse.

Denture cleaner

2 tbsp coconut oil
2 tbsp baking soda
5 drops peppermint essential oil

Mix the coconut oil, baking soda and peppermint oil into a thick paste (softening the coconut oil in a warm place, if needed).

Using an old toothbrush, scrub the paste into the dentures. Rinse off with hot water.

Liquid laundry detergent

5 ltr water
175 g (6 oz) borax
175 g (6 oz) washing soda
175 g (6 oz) castile soap
15 drops lavender essential oil
60 g (2 oz) coconut oil

Bring 1.5 litres of water to a boil in a large saucepan. Leave to cool for 2–3 minutes then add the borax and washing soda. Stir to dissolve.

In a large bucket, mix the remaining water with the castile soap. Add the lavender essential oil to the bucket.

Add the coconut oil to the hot borax mixture then immediately pour into the bucket and combine with the water and castile soap.

Pour the mixture into a large storage container and leave to sit for 24–36 hours, until the mixture has gelled.

The detergent may separate; if this happens just stir well to combine. Use 50–75 ml per laundry load.

Tips and ideas

Borax is a naturally occurring mineral. It is available from hardware shops and online.

Kitchen

Kitchens seem to need so many different types of cleaners for different surfaces and equipment. Not any more – stock up on coconut oil and you'll be able to clean the kitchen and its contents with just one jar.

Chopping board conditioner

Use coconut oil to condition your wooden chopping boards. Apply coconut oil to the board with a piece of kitchen paper and rub into the grain.

Food container stain repellent

Apply a thin layer of coconut oil to your plastic food containers to act as a barrier between the plastic and the food and prevent staining.

Fresh eggs for longer

Eggs can be kept fresher with just a thin layer of coconut oil. Gently apply a layer of coconut oil to the eggshell to act as a protective film, reducing the air coming into contact with the porous shell.

Baking tray treatment

If you find food is burnt and caked onto your baking trays, use a dab of coconut oil to soften the hardened food and remove it more easily. Apply the coconut oil and leave it for a few minutes before scraping off the food.

Prevent freezer burn

Add a layer of coconut oil on top of frozen foods to prevent freezer burn. Coconut oil will provide a protective coating to keep freezing air out of contact with the food. Try melting the coconut oil first and pouring on top of previously frozen sauces. The coconut oil will instantly become solid and will be easy to remove in one piece before defrosting.

Cast-iron seasoning

Use coconut oil straight from the jar to season your cast-iron pan. This will keep it rust free and working well.

Firstly, clean the pan with warm, soapy water. Usually you wouldn't use water and soap on a cast-iron pan but this is fine, as it's about to be seasoned.

Make sure the pan is very dry and apply a thin layer of coconut oil all over the pan, inside and out.

Preheat the oven to 165°C (325°F). Place the pan upside down on a shelf in the oven with a sheet of foil underneath to catch any drips.

Bake in the oven for 1 hour, then turn off the oven and leave the pan inside to cool completely.

Garden and car

It's not just inside the house that coconut oil is essential – move into the garden and you'll find plenty of uses for it here, too. From cleaning the grill to coating snow shovels, the uses are endless.

Fire starters

Make your own fire starters using coconut oil: lightly soak cotton wool balls in melted coconut oil then store safely in a glass jar. When needed, use one of the cotton balls to help fuel your fire.

Grill cleaner

Use coconut oil to remove areas of burnt or caked-on food, or even add a layer of coconut oil to the base of a grill before using. This will make it easier to lift off food, grease and dirt afterwards.

Garden tools conditioner

Condition your garden tools using a thin layer of coconut oil to protect them from becoming rusty.

Keep your mower grass free

Add a layer of coconut oil to the inside of the grass collector on your lawn mower to stop the grass getting stuck to the inside. The layer of coconut oil should make it easy for the cut grass to slide off.

Coat snow shovels

Spread a thin layer of coconut oil on your snow shovel before moving snow – the snow will slide right off.

Lubricate bicycle chains

Use coconut oil as a lubricant on your bicycle chain to keep it from sticking. Simply smear on the oil as needed.

Lubricate motor and moving parts

Use coconut oil as a lubricant for the motor and other moving parts in your car engine.

Dashboard polish

Polish your dashboard with coconut oil to help keep it dust free.

Kids

If you're not keen on the potent head lice treatments on the market, try the more natural application of coconut oil for the same results. And how about letting the patient play with coconut play dough while you're treating their hair?

Head lice treatment

Head lice aren't great fans of coconut oil. The texture of the oil suffocates and removes head lice and their eggs, making it the perfect all-natural head lice treatment.

Melt between 100–220 g (3½–7 oz) of coconut oil (depending on length of hair) in a double boiler.

Ensure the oil is warm (but not hot) before applying to the scalp and the entire length of the hair. Cover the hair with a shower cap and leave for 2–4 hours before shampooing.

Finish with a rinse of 125 ml (4½ fl oz) of apple cider vinegar mixed with 125 ml (4½ fl oz) of water. Don't rinse out, as the smell of the vinegar will subside when the hair dries! It also gives the hair a lovely shine.

Repeat the process until all the lice are gone.

Play dough

Most children's play dough is made with an array of chemicals. This homemade version includes coconut oil, alongside other natural, non-toxic ingredients for safe and fun playtime.

125 g (4½ oz) plain flour
2 tbsp fractionated coconut oil
150 g (5 oz) table salt
2 tbsp cream of tartar
350 ml (12 fl oz) water

Mix the flour, coconut oil, salt and cream of tartar together in a large bowl.

Bring the water to the boil, adding any essential oils or colourings to the water (see variations). Add the water to the bowl, stirring continuously, until it becomes a combined ball of dough.

Leave to cool and then knead it vigorously until it's no longer sticky.

You may need to add a little more flour if this isn't happening after a few minutes of kneading.

Variations

Colour: add drops of food colouring to the water before mixing. For natural shades, add 1 tablespoon of turmeric for yellow; beetroot juice for pink; and matcha green tea powder for green.

Glitter: add 2–4 tablespoons of glitter to the flour at the start of the recipe. This can also be combined with the food colouring variation above.

Scented: to add scent to the play dough, add 5–10 drops of essential oil, such as peppermint or lemon.

Pets

Coconut oil has many benefits for your pet's health on the inside and outside. Take a look at the various ways you can use coconut oil to keep them healthy and happy.

Hoof oil

Coconut oil makes a great conditioner for horses' hooves, keeping them moisturised and shiny.

Ear cleaner

Use coconut oil as a gentle and natural ear cleaner for your pets. Use a small amount of coconut oil on a soft cloth and wipe around the outer ear to clean it.

Nose oil

Keep your pets' noses moisturised with coconut oil to prevent them drying out and becoming cracked. Apply a thin layer of coconut oil and repeat as needed.

Worm treatment

Using coconut oil internally can be a very effective way to expel worms from your pet's body. Simply give them a spoonful of coconut oil neat every day until the parasites have been treated.

Dog shampoo

250 ml (9 fl oz) water
250 ml (9 fl oz) liquid castile soap
60 g (2 oz) fractionated coconut oil
5 drops lemon essential oil

Combine the ingredients in a large jar with a tight-fitting lid. Store in a cool place.

Shake well before use.

Brewers' yeast dog treats for flea prevention

Brewers' yeast is an inactive form of yeast often used as a dietary supplement, as it is high in B vitamins. It's known to help prevent fleas in pets due to its high sulphur content, which makes dogs less palatable to these pests.

225 g (8 oz) coconut oil
60 g (2 oz) brewers' yeast

Melt the coconut oil in a double boiler and pour into a food processor or blender along with the brewers' yeast.

Blend together and pour the mixture into a silicone mould.

Leave to harden in the fridge then pop out of the mould and store in an airtight container.

Offer one treat to your pet per day to keep them flea free.

Peanut butter dog treats for a shiny coat

100 g (3½ oz) coconut oil
125 g (4½ oz) smooth peanut butter
(with no added sugar)

Melt the coconut oil in a double boiler and mix together with the peanut butter until incorporated.

Pour the mixture into silicone moulds and refrigerate until solid.

Store in the fridge, offering one to your pet as needed.

Tips and ideas

Coconut oil can help your dog's skin and hair stay supple and shiny, especially when combined with the treat, peanut butter.

Beauty

JUST AS IT IS important to be aware of what we put in our bodies, it's also important to be aware of what we put on our skin. While many of us have embraced a healthier diet, we've also come to embrace a healthier beauty routine and no better ingredient exists to support that than coconut oil.

When used on the skin coconut oil is easily absorbed and is moisturising and hydrating while also offering antibacterial and antifungal benefits. The antioxidant content helps to protect the skin against free radicals that cause damage and aging.

It is also an excellent cleanser, breaking down both water- and oil-based products like make-up. Its moisturising properties make it not only suitable for use on the skin but also on hair, nails and lips.

Using oils on the skin was once thought to create even oilier skin but the reverse is now known to be true. In fact, the use of natural oils on the skin has shown to reduce oil and breakouts when applied correctly. Another useful property of coconut oil is its ability to form a film or protective barrier over the skin, thus making it perfect for locking in moisture.

Used as an ingredient in a preparation it provides the ideal staple base or carrier oil and is perfect for use in bars, lotions, creams and soaps, as it will not go rancid. When most commercially available beauty products contain chemicals, coconut oil offers an affordable and completely natural chemical-free alternative with an incredible number of uses.

Cleansing cream and make-up remover

If you want to use coconut oil to cleanse your skin daily, you might like to try one of the following coconut oil-based cleansing blends for different skin types – dry, oil or combination.

Essential oils

Many of these preparations use common essential oils. Measurements of essential oils are given in ranges, as the intensity of different brands can vary. Feel free to smell and test the preparation on your skin as you are making it. Essential oils can be very potent so don't use them directly on the skin – coconut oil is an excellent carrier oil.

When rose oil is stated as an ingredient, it's worth noting that rose absolute is more intense than rose otto oil due to the differences in oil extraction.

Basic cleanser

Use 1 teaspoon of pure coconut oil to cleanse the face. Just pour onto cotton wool or cleansing pads.

Blended oil cleansers

To cleanse skin using the following oil blends, mix the oils together in your hands until the coconut oil has softened, then massage gently into your face and neck.

To remove, soak a face cloth in warm water, squeeze out the excess water and gently rub over the skin to remove the excess oil and make-up.

Blends

Olive oil (for dry skin): combine ½ teaspoon of olive oil with ½ teaspoon of coconut oil.

Jojoba (anti-inflammatory): combine ½ teaspoon of jojoba oil with ½ teaspoon of coconut oil.

Tea tree (for oily skin): add 1–2 drops tea tree essential oil to 1 teaspoon of coconut oil.

Avocado (nourishing): combine ½ teaspoon of avocado oil with ½ teaspoon of coconut oil.

Hazelnut (for oily skin): combine ½ teaspoon of hazelnut oil with 1 teaspoon of coconut oil.

Make-up remover

One of the simplest ways to use coconut oil in your beauty regime is as a make-up remover. Coconut oil is an excellent cleanser, as the oil breaks down other oils, as well as water-based products, helping to remove them from the skin.

Take ½ tablespoon of coconut oil and rub between your hands until melted. Gently massage the coconut oil into your face and neck for 1–2 minutes.

To remove, soak a face cloth in warm water, squeeze out the excess water and gently rub over the skin to remove the excess oil.

Eye make-up remover

Place ¼ teaspoon of coconut oil on a cotton pad. Gently wipe the pad across the eyelid area to soften the make-up. Soak a clean cotton pad in warm water and use to remove excess oil and make-up. Repeat with the other eye.

Face masks

Sometimes skin needs extra pampering and face masks are a great way to give some intensive nourishment. Here are a number of preparations that include coconut oil and other ingredients for exfoliating, hydrating, nourishing and energising treatments.

Nourishing and clarifying honey face mask

1 tsp honey
1 tsp coconut oil

Combine the ingredients in a small bowl (soften the coconut oil in a warm place, if needed) and apply directly to clean skin, avoiding sensitive areas like the eyes.

Leave for 10–15 minutes then remove with a soft face cloth steeped in warm water.

Ultra-hydrating avocado face mask

½ ripe avocado
1 tbsp coconut oil

Mash the avocado with the coconut oil until the mixture is really smooth (soften the coconut oil in a warm place, if needed).

Immediately apply the mask to the face – avoiding sensitive areas such as the eyes – and leave on for 10–15 minutes.

Remove using cotton pads and finish by removing any residue with a face cloth steeped in warm water.

Oat exfoliating face mask

½ tbsp steel cut or porridge oats (not jumbo oats)
1 tbsp coconut oil

Combine the oats with the coconut oil (soften the coconut oil in a warm place, if needed).

Apply to the face, avoiding sensitive areas like the eyes, and leave on for 5–10 minutes.

To remove, begin by gently massaging the mask into the skin for a light exfoliating sensation. Remove with a cotton pad and then remove any residue using a face cloth steeped in warm water.

Matcha green tea energising face mask

1 tsp matcha green tea powder
½ tbsp coconut oil

Combine the ingredients until a paste has formed. Spread the paste on the skin and leave for 5–10 minutes (remove if there are any signs of irritation).

Remove with a face cloth steeped in warm water.

Tips and ideas

Matcha green tea is another modern miracle ingredient. It's made from finely powdered green tea leaves, which are rich in antioxidants, as well as a small amount of caffeine. Caffeine has benefits for skin, including skin damage repair and circulation promotion, which makes this mask especially energising.

Facial creams and oils

Coconut oil is an amazing hydrator and moisturiser for skin. It has a natural SPF 4 rating, is full of antioxidants to protect the skin and its antibacterial properties can help prevent breakouts. When combined with certain essential oils, the result is a soft cream that is perfect for your daily routine.

Facial moisturiser

150 g (5 oz) coconut oil
1–2 capsules vitamin E oil
125 g (4½ oz) aloe vera

Melt the coconut oil in a double boiler. Empty the contents of the vitamin E capsules into the oil and add the selected essential oils (see below) and aloe vera.

Using an electric mixer, beat the coconut oil mixture until it becomes creamy.

Store in a small jar for up to 3 months.

Variations

Anti-aging: add 10–20 drops of frankincense essential oil.

Oily skin: add 10–20 drops of tea tree essential oil.

Dry skin: add 10–20 drops of rose essential oil.

Anti-aging serum

60 g (2 oz) coconut oil
5–10 drops frankincense essential oil
5–10 drops rose essential oil

Melt the coconut oil in a double boiler and add the essential oils. Mix gently to combine.

Pour the coconut oil into a small jar and leave in a cool place to harden.

To apply, smear some of the serum onto your fingers and melt between your hands before massaging into your face and neck.

Shaving

Coconut oil offers the perfect combination of moisturisation and lubrication for shaving. As well as using it directly, it can be combined with other ingredients to create a rich, thick shaving cream.

Shaving oil

Coconut oil can be used as a soothing shaving oil. Simply melt the coconut oil between your hands and apply a layer to the desired area of the skin before shaving. Repeat as needed.

Basic shaving cream

100 g (3½ oz) coconut oil
60 g (2 oz) shea butter
60 g (2 oz) olive oil

Melt the coconut oil and shea butter together in a double boiler. Once melted, stir in the olive oil.

Place in a refrigerator until the mixture is no longer a liquid but more of a solid, creamy consistency.

Beat the mixture with a stand or electric mixer until stiff peaks form.

Transfer to a jar or airtight container and store in a cool place.

Variations

Citrus/musk: gradually add 10–20 drops each of eucalyptus and lemongrass essential oils, while whipping the cream, testing the intensity of the scent as you go.

Floral: gradually add 10–20 drops each of lavender and rose essential oils, while whipping the cream, testing the intensity of the scent as you go.

Beard balm

To keep a beard shiny, moisturised and neat, beard balm can be applied. Coconut oil forms the base for this lightly scented balm.

Cedarwood beard balm

60 g (2 oz) coconut oil
2 tbsp beeswax
5–10 drops cedarwood essential oil

Melt the coconut oil and beeswax in a double boiler. Add the essential oil and pour into a tin or small jar. Leave to harden.

Apply balm as needed and store in a cool place.

Soaps and scrubs

Keep hands clean and moisturised with this liquid hand soap that contains no toxic ingredients and smells amazing. Coconut oil's texture works well as a carrier for exfoliating, while adding its own incredible moisturising benefits. Here are several ways to use coconut oil as a body scrub.

Foaming hand soap

2 tbsp castile soap
1 tsp fractionated coconut oil
4 drops lemon essential oil
4 drops orange essential oil

Place the castile soap, coconut oil and essential oils in a bottle with a foaming-action pump lid.

Top up the bottle with boiled and cooled water. Shake before dispensing the foam.

Cuticle oil

Coconut oil makes a fantastic cuticle treatment. Simply apply coconut oil to the cuticle area and massage, gently pushing the skin back from the nails.

Coffee grinds scrub

75 g (2½ oz) cup coconut oil
100–150 g (3½–5 oz) old coffee grinds
   (from a coffee press or similar)
5–10 drops vanilla oil (optional)

Melt the coconut oil in a double boiler and stir in the coffee grinds and vanilla oil (if using).

Transfer to a jar or airtight container and leave for at least 3 hours for the caffeine to infuse the oil. You may wish to warm the scrub to a liquid state before using.

Store any leftover scrub in a cool, dark place for up to 1 week.

Basic body wash

125 ml (4½ fl oz) liquid castile soap
2 tbsp fractionated coconut oil
1 tbsp jojoba oil
2 capsules vitamin E oil

Combine all the ingredients in a bottle or jar. Shake well before use.

Variations

Citrus: add 10–20 drops of lemon essential oil and 10–20 drops of orange essential oil.

Rose: add 20–40 drops of rose essential oil.

Mint: add 5–10 drops of eucalyptus essential oil and 10–20 drops of peppermint essential oil.

Moisturising: replace jojoba oil with avocado oil.

Cinnamon and ginger: add 10–20 drops of cinnamon essential oil and 5–10 drops of ginger essential oil.

You can experiment with the amount of essential oils in your preparation, depending on how intensely you'd like the body wash to be scented.

Lemon body scrub

75 g (2½ oz) coconut oil
75–100 g (2½–3½ oz) sugar
10 drops lemon essential oil
Juice of 1 lemon

This citrus-scented scrub is excellent for energising and stimulating the skin.

Melt the coconut oil in a double boiler and stir in the sugar, lemon essential oil and lemon juice.

The scrub can be used immediately. If left and solidified, you may wish to warm the scrub back to a liquid state.

Store any leftover scrub in a cool, dark place for up to 1 week.

Lavender body scrub

75 g (2½ oz) coconut oil
75–100 g (2½–3½ oz) sugar
2–3 tbsp dried lavender buds
  and/or 10 drops lavender
  essential oil

This fragrant lavender scrub is perfect to use before bed or whenever you need a little relaxation.

Melt the coconut oil in a double boiler and stir in the sugar and lavender flowers or essential oil.

The scrub can be used immediately. If left and solidified, you may wish to warm the scrub back to a liquid state.

Store any leftover scrub in a cool, dark place for up to 1 week.

Pink rose salt body scrub

75 g (2½ oz) coconut oil
100–150 g (3½–5 oz) fine
  Himalayan pink salt
10–20 drops rose essential oil
40 g (1½ oz) dried rose petals
  (optional)

Melt the coconut oil in a double boiler and stir in the salt, rose essential oil and dried rose petals (if using).

The scrub can be used immediately. If left and solidified, you may wish to warm the scrub back to a liquid state.

Store any leftover scrub in a cool, dark place for up to 1 week.

Lime and mint body scrub

75 g (2½ oz) coconut oil
75–100 g (2½–3½ oz) sugar
Juice of 1 lime
5–10 drops lime essential oil
3–5 drops peppermint essential oil

This refreshing scented scrub is ideal for using in the morning to help with alertness and energy.

Melt the coconut oil in a double boiler and stir in the sugar, lime juice and essential oils.

The scrub can be used immediately. If left and solidified, you may wish to warm the scrub back to a liquid state.

Store any leftover scrub in a cool, dark place for up to 1 week.

Salt foot scrub

75 g (2½ oz) coconut oil
75–100 g (2½–3½ oz) rock salt
10–20 drops peppermint
    essential oil

The hard skin on the feet benefits from a rougher exfoliating agent, alongside the softening properties of coconut oil.

Melt the coconut oil in a double boiler and stir in the salt and peppermint oil.

The scrub can be used immediately. If left and solidified, you may wish to warm the scrub back to a liquid state.

Store any leftover scrub in a cool, dark place for up to 1 week.

Tips and ideas

Rock salt is another name for the rock halite. The large granules make it the perfect ingredient for foot scrubs and other exfoliating beauty products.

Body lotions and butters

When it comes to pampering, coconut oil is the perfect partner. With just a few additional ingredients you can create a range of moisturising, hydrating and aromatic treats for your skin.

Body lotion bar

Lotion bars make a good alternative to moisturising creams. This is a rich lotion in solid form: the bar can be rubbed directly on to the skin or rubbed between your hands and the melted lotion then massaged into the skin.

100 g (3½ oz) coconut oil
25 g (1 oz) shea butter
60 g (2 oz) beeswax
40 g (1½ oz) almond oil or olive oil

Melt the coconut oil, shea butter and beeswax in a double boiler. Stir in the almond oil and any essential oils you'd like to use.

Carefully pour the mix into a silicone mould (a silicone muffin tin works well) and leave to cool.

Store in a cool place.

Body butter

This is undoubtedly one of the most wonderful ways to use coconut oil on your skin and it's also very easy to make. Body butter is a lotion with a rich, thick, and luxuriously creamy texture that is perfect for hydrating dry skin.

225 g (8 oz) coconut oil
100 g (3½ oz) cocoa butter

Melt the coconut oil and cocoa butter in a double boiler. Pour into a mixing bowl and refrigerate until it's in a semi-solid state.

Whip the mixture using a stand mixer or electric hand mixer until thick and creamy. Add any essential oils while whipping the mixture.

Transfer to a jar or airtight container and store at room temperature.

Variations

Rose: add 20–40 drops of rose essential oil.

Relaxing blend: add 10 drops of lavender essential oil, 10 drops ylang ylang and 10 drops of bergamot essential oil.

Jojoba: add 2 tablespoons of jojoba oil before whipping; this will create a softer and lighter consistency.

Shea: replace half the cocoa butter with the same amount of shea butter.

Ginger and lime: add 10 drops of ginger essential oil and 20 drops of lime essential oil.

Aloe vera: add 125 g (4½ oz) of aloe vera gel after the initial mixture has been whipped, then whip again. The butter will be lighter.

Massage oils and skin treatments

Coconut oil – extra virgin, virgin or fractionated – is excellent for massages, while also being suitable as a carrier for essential oils. Here are two blends for relaxation and energising, as well as some coconut oil-based treatments for common skin conditions.

Relaxing massage oil

100 g (3½ oz) coconut oil (liquid fractionated oil
  or solid virgin oil)
5–10 drops lavender essential oil
5–10 drops geranium essential oil
5–10 drops ylang ylang essential oil

Mix the coconut oil with the essential oils. If using fractionated coconut oil, transfer to a bottle; if using virgin coconut oil, transfer to a jar.

To use the virgin coconut massage oil, scoop out the solid oil blend and melt between your hands before massaging.

Energising massage oil

100 g (3½ oz) coconut oil (liquid fractionated oil
  or solid virgin oil)
10 drops lemon essential oil
5 drops orange essential oil
10 drops cedarwood essential oil

Mix the coconut oil with the essential oils. If using fractionated coconut oil, transfer to a bottle; if using virgin coconut oil, transfer to a jar.

To use the virgin coconut massage oil, scoop out the solid oil blend and melt between the hands before massaging.

Age spot lightener

1 tbsp coconut oil
1 tbsp lemon juice
1 capsule vitamin E oil

Soften the coconut oil in a warm place and whisk in the lemon juice (it will still be slightly separated, so mix it in as best you can).

Empty the oil from the vitamin E capsule and add to the mixture.

Apply to age spots and allow the mixture to be absorbed. Repeat as needed.

Cellulite treatment

This easy-to-create cellulite treatment makes use of grapefruit essential oil. Its anti-inflammatory compounds can help to break down cellulite.

100 g (3½ oz) coconut oil
20 drops grapefruit essential oil

Melt the coconut oil in a double boiler and add the grapefruit oil. Transfer to a jar to harden.

To apply, scoop out some of the balm and massage directly into areas with cellulite.

Deodorant and perfume

Coconut oil's antibacterial properties inhibit the growth of bacteria that create unpleasant odours, while also moisturising delicate underarm skin. Many standard deodorants contain chemical ingredients that can block the sweat glands. The following preparations are completely natural but still effective.

Deodorant

2 tbsp shea butter
1 tbsp cocoa butter
2 tbsp coconut oil (see tip below)
3 tbsp baking soda
2 tbsp cornstarch
2 vitamin E capsules
20 drops lemongrass or tea tree essential oil

Melt the shea butter, cocoa butter and coconut oil in a double boiler. Stir in the baking soda and cornstarch. Add the oil from the vitamin E capsules and add the lemongrass or tea tree essential oil.

Transfer to a jar, airtight container or deodorant tube. To apply, scoop out a little of the cream and apply to the underarm area.

As this is a completely natural product, it won't prevent you from sweating, as it doesn't clog up your sweat glands but it will manage unpleasant odours.

Perfume

2 tbsp coconut oil
2 tbsp beeswax
20–40 drops essential oil blend (see below)

Melt the coconut oil and beeswax in a double boiler and add the essential oils. Pour into a small tin or glass jar and leave to cool and solidify.

To apply, simply rub a small amount of the solid perfume on your pulse points.

Blends

Here are some ideas for blends of essential oils to create perfume scents but you can also experiment and create your own. Test while adding the oils by dabbing a little of the liquid mixture onto your wrist.

Citrus: lemon, orange, lemongrass.

Sensual: jasmine, rose, ylang ylang.

Fresh: lime, lemongrass, cedarwood.

Floral: lavender, geranium.

Tips and ideas

If you live in a cooler climate and would like to use the deodorant from a jar, use fractionated coconut oil in place of 1 tablespoon of the virgin coconut oil to create a slightly less solid texture. However, if you are using a deodorant tube, use all virgin coconut oil to keep it solid.

Lip balms and toothpaste

Cold or dry weather can make lips become dry and cracked. These natural preparations will help to protect and moisturise your lips all year round.

Coconut oil and brown sugar lip scrub

Coconut oil is ideal for keeping lips soft. Here are several ways to use it, from removing dry, chapped skin to keeping lips soft and supple.

½ tbsp coconut oil
1 tsp soft brown sugar

Soften the coconut oil in a warm place and mix with the brown sugar.

Apply to the lips in circular motions to gently scrub away rough skin. Wipe off the scrub with a cloth.

Minty fresh lip scrub

½ tbsp coconut oil
1 tsp sugar
2 drops peppermint essential oil

Soften the coconut oil in a warm place and mix with the sugar and peppermint essential oil.

Apply to the lips in circular motions, gently scrubbing away rough skin. Wipe off the scrub with a cloth.

Peppermint lip balm

2 tbsp coconut oil
2 tbsp beeswax
5 drops peppermint essential oil

Soften the coconut oil and beeswax in a warm place. Add the peppermint essential oil and combine.

Pour into small tins or a small jar and leave to cool and harden.

Tinted lip balm

This is a great way to give new life to an old lipstick!

2 tbsp coconut oil
2 tbsp beeswax
Old lipstick in any color

Soften the coconut oil and beeswax in a warm place. Add a small piece of the lipstick, crushed with the back of a spoon. Mix well into the warm liquid.

Pour into small tins or a small jar and leave to cool and harden.

Cocoa vanilla lip balm

2 tbsp coconut oil
2 tbsp beeswax
2 tbsp cocoa butter
5–10 drops vanilla oil

Soften the coconut oil and beeswax in a warm place. Add the cocoa butter and vanilla oil and mix well into the liquid.

Pour into small tins or a small jar and leave to cool and harden.

Tips and ideas

To keep your lip balm in a solid state, keep it in the refrigerator.

Toothpaste

Using coconut oil for your teeth may seem a little unusual but it works well in homemade, toxin-free toothpaste and teeth whitener. This toothpaste combines the benefits of coconut oil with the cleaning properties of baking soda and the oral health benefits of xylitol – a natural sweetener. Xylitol sweetens toothpaste and prevents bacteria from sticking to the teeth and gums.

3 tbsp coconut oil
1 tbsp baking soda
1 tbsp xylitol (optional)
10 drops peppermint essential oil

Combine all the ingredients, softening the coconut oil in a warm place, if needed. Store in a small jar or airtight container.

To use, dip the bristles of your toothbrush into the paste and use as you would a regular toothpaste.

Teeth whitener

Don't be put off by the yellow colour of the turmeric! Although bright, it is an excellent teeth whitener and a much healthier alternative to chemical-filled teeth-whitening strips. It also has a range of benefits to oral health, including being a potent anti-inflammatory, perfect for protecting gum health.

1 tbsp coconut oil
½ tsp turmeric
1–2 drops peppermint essential oil (optional)

Combine the coconut oil, turmeric and peppermint oil (if using) into a thick paste.

Spread the mixture over the teeth and leave to work for 3–5 minutes before rinsing and spitting out (in the bin rather than down the sink).

Repeat daily until you see the desired result.

Foot cream

If one part of our body often requires a little extra attention it's our feet. They can be prone to hard, dry skin and aches and pains, as well as fungal infections. This foot cream will moisturise feet, while the coconut oil helps to protect against infections. The essential oils will help them feel refreshed after a busy day.

60 g (2 oz) coconut oil
25 g (1 oz) shea butter
2 capsules vitamin E

Melt the coconut oil and shea butter in a double boiler. Squeeze the oil from the vitamin E capsules into the mixture. Leave to cool until the oils are no longer liquid but aren't fully solidified.

Whip the oils with a stand mixer or electric mixer until thick and creamy. Add the essential oils (if using) while you whip.

Transfer the cream to a jar or airtight container and store in a cool place.

Variations

Peppermint: add 20–30 drops of peppermint essential oil.

Lemon: add 20–30 drops of lemon essential oil.

Hair

Coconut oil is a wonderful treatment for all hair types but is especially beneficial for dry or damaged hair. Here are several ways to use it to condition, detangle and treat your hair.

Hair serum

Use coconut oil neat as a hair serum. Melt a tiny amount between your fingers and use it to tame any frizz on dry hair.

Hair detangler

Apply plain coconut oil to knots and tangles and gently tease it out with a comb. Shampoo and condition as normal.

Split end treatment

Use coconut oil straight from the jar as a split end treatment. Massage it into the ends of the hair and leave overnight to moisturise the hair shaft. Shampoo and condition your hair as normal the following day.

Coconut milk shampoo

60 g (2 oz) canned coconut milk
25 g (1 oz) castile soap
1 tsp fractionated coconut oil
5–10 drops essential oil of choice

Combine all the ingredients in a bottle or jar. To use, shake well and apply 1 teaspoon to wet hair and massage in well. Rinse and use conditioner, if required.

The shampoo will keep for 3–4 weeks in a cool place in the bathroom.

Deep conditioner

2–4 tbsp coconut oil (depending on hair length)
1 tbsp olive oil or avocado oil
5 drops essential oil of choice

Soften the coconut oil and combine with the olive or avocado oil and essential oil.

Gently massage into the length of the hair and scalp. Cover the hair with a shower cap or cling film and leave the conditioner to work for up to 30 minutes.

Rinse well and shampoo and condition as normal.

Avocado hair mask

2 tbsp coconut oil
1 tsp honey
1 avocado

Soften the coconut oil in a warm place and add to a blender or food processor with the honey. Scoop the flesh from the avocado and add to the blender. Blend until smooth.

Apply the mask to the hair and scalp and leave for 10–15 minutes before rinsing. Shampoo and condition as normal.

Banana and yogurt hair mask

1 banana
60 g (2 oz) natural yogurt
2 tbsp coconut oil

Mash the banana and yogurt together in a bowl until no lumps of banana remain (you could use a blender or food processor). Soften the coconut oil and mix into the banana and yogurt.

Apply to the hair, from the scalp to the ends, and leave for 10–20 minutes. Rinse well and shampoo and condition as normal.

Egg yolk hair mask

1 tbsp coconut oil
1 tbsp olive oil
1 tbsp honey
1 egg yolk (at room temperature)

Soften the coconut oil and whisk with the rest of the ingredients.

Apply to the hair and leave for 10–15 minutes. Rinse well and shampoo and condition as normal.

Tips and ideas

After applying the hair mask, cover the scalp and hair with a layer of cling film. This will help to warm the scalp and increase the benefits of the mask.

Bath

Coconut oil makes a rich, nourishing addition to your bath, adding skin-softening benefits. These soaks, melts and bath bombs use essential oils, honey, dried flowers and other natural ingredients for extra indulgence.

Milk and honey bath soak

60 g (2 oz) coconut oil
60 g (2 oz) canned coconut milk
2 tbsp honey

This simple addition to your bath will leave your skin feeling nourished and softened.

Melt the coconut oil in a double boiler and combine with the coconut milk and honey.

Pour directly into a warm bath to enjoy the benefits.

Rose bath bombs

250 g (9 oz) citric acid
250 g (9 oz) baking soda
60 g (2 oz) cornstarch
100 g (3½ oz) coconut oil
10 drops rose essential oil
40 g (1½ oz) dried rose petals or buds (optional)
2–3 tbsp beetroot juice or natural food coloring (optional)

For a fun addition to your bath, try one of these bath bombs.

Combine all the ingredients in a glass bowl until they have a sand-like texture. Pack the mixture into silicone moulds or create round bundles of the mix by wrapping in cling film.

Leave for at least 24 hours to harden and dry out before removing. The bath bombs should be completely dry before using.

Bath melts

100 g (3½ oz) coconut oil
2 tbsp dried rose petals or lavender buds
20 drops rose or lavender essential oil

A bath melt is a lovely way to add essential oils and skin-softening coconut oil to your bath.

Melt the coconut oil in a double boiler and add your choice of rose petals and rose essential oil, or lavender buds and lavender essential oil. Pour into a silicone mould and leave to harden.

Store the bath melts in a jar, in a cool place in the bathroom and add to your bath, as desired.

Variation

Cocoa butter bath melts: replace the dried flowers and essential oil with 25 g (1 oz) of cocoa butter and 5–10 drops of vanilla essential oil.

Sleepy time bath oil

100 g (3½ oz) fractionated coconut oil
10–15 drops lavender essential oil
5–10 drops cedarwood essential oil

Combine all the ingredients in a bottle.
Use 1–2 tablespoons per bath, as required.

Moisturising vanilla bath oil

100 g (3½ oz) fractionated coconut oil
2 tbsp avocado oil
10–20 drops vanilla oil

Combine all the ingredients in a bottle.
Use 1–2 tablespoons per bath, as required.

Uplifting lemon and lime bath oil

100 g (3½ oz) fractionated coconut oil
10–20 drops lemon essential oil
10–20 drops lime essential oil

Combine all the ingredients in a bottle.
Use 1–2 tablespoons per bath, as required.

De-stress blend bath oil

100 g (3½ oz) fractionated coconut oil
20 drops lavender essential oil
10 drops frankincense essential oil

Combine all the ingredients in a bottle.
Use 1–2 tablespoons per bath, as required.

Make-up

Coconut oil is an ideal ingredient in homemade make-up. The antibacterial properties keep preparations fresh and stop the transfer of bacteria, as well as providing hydration to the skin.

Brow gel

Coconut oil can be used straight from the jar to tame unruly eyebrows. Simply brush a little oil through them to keep them in place.

Eyelash gel

Coconut oil is excellent for the eyelashes, keeping them moisturised and protected. Use your index finger to gently apply coconut oil to the eyelashes for added definition.

Shimmer or glitter gel

2 tbsp coconut oil
1 tbsp shimmer powder
or 1–2 tbsp fine glitter

Melt the coconut oil by moving to a warm place and mix with the powder or glitter. Pour into a small jar and leave to harden.

Apply to the skin with fingertips or a make-up brush.

The shimmer or glitter gel will keep for up to 1 month, if stored in a cool place.

Eyeliner

2 tsp coconut oil
For black eyeliner: ½ tsp activated charcoal
For brown eyeliner: ½ tsp cocoa powder

Melt the coconut oil by moving to a warm place and combine with either the charcoal or cocoa powder. Place the mixture in a small tin or jar and leave to harden.

Apply with a stiff eyeliner brush, softening the mixture with some warmth first, if needed.

The eyeliner will keep for up to 2 weeks, if stored in a cool place.

Cheekbone highlighter

Use coconut oil straight from the jar as a cheekbone highlighter. Coconut oil gives skin a natural, dewy glow. Apply a small amount of oil to the cheekbones and blend in.

Index